Project Cost Management

GROUP

Project Cost Management
Principles, Tools, Techniques, and Best Practices for Project Finance

Ray W. Frohnhoefer and Inham Hassen

GROUP

Project Cost Management: Principles, Tools, Techniques, and Best Practices for Project Finance

ISBN-13: 978-1-7356213-1-9 (paperback)
ISBN-13: 978-1-7356213-2-6 (e-book)

Cover design by Luisito C. Pangilinan
Copyediting aided by Microsoft Word and Grammarly
References supported by Zotero
Indexing supported by OpenView Index Generator

For information about copyright, permissions, bulk discounts, or purchase, contact:

PPC Group, LLC
3450 3rd Avenue
Suite 309
San Diego, CA 92103
USA
https://ppcgroup.us
https://accidentalpm.online
http://rayfrohnhoefer.com

About the Author – Ray Frohnhoefer

Ray Frohnhoefer is the Managing Partner of PPC Group, LLC, helping aspiring, new, and accidental project managers and their organizations improve project management practice. Products and services include international bestsellers in Business Project Management, education, corporate training, and consulting.

Ray has led consulting teams in many industries and locations over his 40-year career. Notable projects include:

- rolling out a UNIX development environment to 400+ developers in 16 locations
- testing electronic voting equipment with a team of 30 for San Diego County
- patenting an estimating tool used by a global Project Management Office.

No stranger to virtual, global teams, he has worked with them his entire career.

Ray has had a dual career in project management and training. For eight years, he was an author, editor, and lecturer for the Edison Engineering Advanced Course in Computers. In addition, he has been teaching project management and business analysis classes for UC San Diego's Division of Extended Studies for 18 years.

A long-time Project Management Institute (PMI) volunteer, Ray served as President of the PMI San Diego Chapter in 2005. In 2006 he was the first official PMI Region Mentor for Southwest North America. In addition, he has supported several international PMI committees and groups over the past 15 years. Ray also helped the PMI Educational Foundation create its first professional development scholarship, and he continues to support their work.

Ray holds an undergraduate degree in Mathematics with a Computer Science concentration and an MBA degree in Technology Management. He is a PMI Leadership Institute Master Class (LIMC) graduate and a Certified Computer Professional (CCP).

About the Author – M. Inham Hassen

Inham Hassen became a project manager by accident. Since his project management journey began, he has delivered projects in the UK, Europe, South Asia, the Far East, and Africa. These projects include telecommunications network roll-outs, large-scale post-merger integrations, core banking systems implementations, emergency response programs for COVID-19, and digital transformations.

He has a master's degree in IT Management from Carnegie Mellon University, an LLM in Law from Sunderland University, and an Electrical Engineering degree from the Indian Institute of Technology. Furthermore, he possesses PMP, PRINCE2 Practitioner, MoP Practitioner, P3O Practitioner, and PMO Value Ring Certified Practitioner certifications. In addition to this, he is also an accredited trainer in PRINCE2 and MoP.

He actively works with the global project management community to enhance the profession. He is a judging committee member of the annual award for the world's best-run project management office (organized by the PMO Global Alliance). Inham is a reviewer for P3.express, a European Commission-funded minimalistic project management methodology, and the author of an MoP Foundation study guide. He created the world's first MoP Foundation exam simulator and the world's first and only Wiki for Project Portfolio Management (MoP.wiki).

He was awarded the Fellowship of the Royal Society of Arts in the UK in 2021.

Dedication

I dedicate this book to my husband, who always supports my work.

And to my readers and fellow project managers, it's a crucial time to increase your skills with a rapidly evolving workplace. Never stop learning.

—Ray

I dedicate this book to

- My teachers at Wesley College, Colombo, Sri Lanka, who are the reason for where I am now.

- My wife for her love, care, and extraordinary ability to tolerate me.

—Inham

Table of Contents

List of Figures, Tables, and Equations

Preface

Much like my previous books, this book is based on my career-long work and learning. My interest in cost management and finance started in the late 70s when a proposed project was turned down. Management explained that the company would not invest in a product provided at no charge to clients. I consulted with our Finance Department to find that were it not for this free product, nearly two-thirds of the company's revenue would evaporate. I learned this was known as "pull-through revenue." The project was approved with this discovery.

This incident sparked my interest, and I signed up for a program to be trained as a company auditor while still managing projects. Unfortunately, it was not for the position but because many of the clients I supported with software projects were financial institutions. Ironic since I had no budget responsibility this early in my project management career. I worked exclusively with human resources, so management interest was in time. The Finance Department managed most of the actual budgets.

In 1990, due to a mistake by senior management, I had the opportunity to set and manage a modest project budget. This work and previous experiences later enabled me to manage projects related to insurance companies, the integration and implementation of PeopleSoft Financials, and other financial software projects throughout the 90s. I completed an MBA in 2000 with a minor in Finance.

Then, starting in 2003 and for about 17 years, I did a class for UC San Diego's Division of Extended Studies titled Controlling Project Costs and Risks. It underwent rewrites roughly four times in that period and later became known as Project Cost and Risk Management. Cost management was consistently about a third of the material, focusing primarily on creating and managing project budgets.

In 2020, I split the course into two, doubling the content for cost and risk. That was easy to do for risk as I had just finished *Risk Assessment Framework: Successfully Navigating Uncertainty* in 2019. However, I never had a text for cost management, so I sought out possibilities. I found books dedicated to industries or portions of cost management. For example:

- Construction projects
- Cost control
- Cost from an accounting viewpoint
- Cost from the Association for the Advancement of Cost Engineering viewpoint

I also found that the primary place where cost management in project selection is covered is in PMP review books. Unfortunately, there has only been one book in the last five to ten years "comprehensive" concerning project cost management. Still, it is very short and mostly echoes the PMBOK Guide with little "how-to" information.

After reviewing these sources, I developed an expanded outline and the course. I added material on cost and project initiation, cash flow management (critical for many construction projects), and expanded on existing cost control material.

My goal has always been to fill in the critical knowledge areas beyond the Accidental Project Management books. So, in 2021, I started to work on further expanding my course outline into a full-length text. That year I also partnered with Inham Hassen. Inham has strong management and editing skills and brings a PMO and international perspective to the book. I'm honored to work with him to complete this book.

This book aims to be clear enough for the accidental, new, or aspiring project manager to understand but sufficiently comprehensive for experienced project managers (similar to the *Risk Assessment Framework*). We believe we broadly cover all aspects of cost management and fill in the voids left by spotty coverage with few new and significant books in the field. Like other PPC Group books, tips and templates support the text.

I hope you enjoy this book as much as we have enjoyed working on it!

- **Ray W. Frohnhoefer**
San Diego, California, USA
May 2022

Acknowledgments

So many people are involved with this book that the best way to start is, "We're sorry if we have left out your name."

First, we would like to thank Dr. John Estrella. John is an incredible business coach and mentor – all of us who work with him have experienced extraordinary transformations in our businesses. Without John's guidance, this book would probably still be an idea.

Next, we'd like to thank the many global professionals who have helped by reading, editing, or giving feedback and guidance for this book: Chuck Adams (USA), Shaham Anam (Sweden), Shweta Brahmakshatriya (India), Naomi Caietti (USA), John Estrella (Canada), Sumith Kahanda (Canada), Nitin Kundeshwar (USA), Deasún Ó Conchúir (Switzerland), Renjith Suresh Padma (India), Harjit Singh (USA), Peeyush Thakur (Canada), Kashif Zafeer (Kuwait).

Finally, we want to thank our colleagues and students who provided information and feedback over time that have gone into the writing of this book.

#PROJECTCOSTMANAGEMENT

INTRODUCTION TO PROJECT COST MANAGEMENT

The project management knowledge area of cost management is concerned with estimating, budgeting, and controlling the budget to stay within the approved expenditures for a project. While it may sound simple, identifying all project costs is perhaps the most challenging task for a project manager and team. In addition to the basic costs of resources, additional charges may stem from economic conditions, equipment operating expenses, loan and bond repayments, and various other expenses.

To effectively estimate, document, and manage costs, project managers must navigate national, state, local, and sometimes international and corporate financial regulations and organizational practices. Therefore, practitioners need the most flexibility in this area and must partner with management and financial professionals to determine the exact extent of their financial roles and responsibilities.

No organization has unlimited financial resources, so project cost management is relevant to all projects, regardless of the management methods used. Predictive[1] or waterfall projects have the most detail available for budgeting. The project schedule and resources inform the costs of each activity or task. Summing these costs together creates the budget - this is a bottom-up approach.

Agile project management methods use less accurate estimation methods and are generally less concerned with costs. The initial budget is often top-down, based on experience and judgment. Steps may be needed to translate estimates in story points to dollars. Those backlog items with higher story points may need a further breakdown to determine costs. The details of charges only become known with each sprint.

Therefore, the project management practitioner must factor in cost goals when determining the project methods. For example, projects with fixed funding or a desire for more robust cost control may require predictive or hybrid (e.g., a combination of predictive, iterative, and agile methods) methods to get the best outcomes. Combining these methods is also significant as predictive methods offer the best opportunities for cost control.

This book aims to provide a comprehensive guide to project cost management for those with a fundamental understanding of project management. Rather than focus on budget alone, this book covers financial concepts for project selection, estimation, payments, financing, and control throughout the project lifecycle. We've made every effort to keep concepts clear for aspiring, new, and accidental

---

[1] If you do not understand fundamental project management terminology, we highly recommend that you read *Accidental Project Manager: Zero to Hero in 7 Days* and/or *Accidental Agile Project Manager: Zero to Hero in 7 Iterations* first. This book builds on the basic project management knowledge presented in these books. Another valuable resource is the *PMI Lexicon of Project Management Terms*.

project managers while covering project financial topics relevant to all project managers.

PART I: COST MANAGEMENT PROCESSES AND PRINCIPLES

"Remember that time is money. He that can earn ten shillings a day by his labour, and goes abroad, or sits idle one half of that day, though he spends but sixpence during his diversion or idleness, it ought not to be reckoned the only expence; he hath really spent or thrown away five shillings besides."

– Benjamin Franklin

CHAPTER 1

PROJECT COST MANAGEMENT PROCESSES

The cost management processes of the PMBOK® Guide are deceptively simple. They aim to create a budget and monitor progress against it. But unfortunately, things aren't always as simple as the project manager may hope in real projects.

Many planning processes impact cost management. For example, it may be challenging to estimate costs without a schedule indicating the timeline for resources. Also, the project manager may have to work with a procurement resource for purchases. Further, large and mega-projects will have financing and payment terms that are difficult to estimate and track.

It is also helpful for the project manager to understand the basics of cost management of portfolios and programs. The understanding will provide insight into management thinking and preferences that will be important for later decision-making. The first section of this book and the chapter, "Project Selection Techniques Using Cost," will help set the stage for cost management at the project level.

Before getting into the "nuts and bolts" of cost management, let's briefly look at each standard process.

Plan Cost Management

The Plan Cost Management process uses the known information about the project to specify how project costs will be managed and controlled. At this point in planning, this is primarily a project charter and an overall project management plan. The PMBOK® Guide outlines the "how" but does not go into sufficient detail to allow you to complete an effective plan.

A reasonable cost management plan is reusable to a large extent. Therefore, having a good one is essential. The chapter, Cost Management Planning, contains a review of the critical and optional components. Further, please see Appendix A for access to a cost management plan template.

Estimate Costs

The Estimate Costs process approximates the cost resources necessary for the project. The best way to do this is to use the Work Breakdown Structure (WBS); however, that isn't the only way.

It is essential to recognize that the project manager should revisit the estimates and the budget throughout the project. The cost represented in the project charter is usually either an executive "guess" or the amount the organization has decided to budget for the project. It isn't easy to achieve accuracy without knowing exactly how the work will be done. Therefore, as project planning progresses, the estimates should be re-visited.

When the WBS is complete is one opportunity. Once the work packages are known, compare their estimates to the initiation estimate. Some long-term projects should be estimated again when more detail is known, such as when the requirements or the project's design is complete. A re-estimate will make sure there are no surprise costs later.

The chapter "Cost Estimation Techniques" will thoroughly cover how to estimate and includes a template for using the PERT estimation technique. PERT is a powerful tool for accurate estimates and answering "what if" questions about the forecast costs. While designed initially for schedule estimates, it is equally applicable to costs.

Determine Budget

Determine Budget aggregates costs into categories and units for financial reporting. The organization or its finance department often sets these categories. The project cost baseline should represent all funds needed to complete the project. At this point, the budget should include contingency reserves. The need for contingency reserves implies that understanding project risks is required since contingency reserves are for identified risks.

While not a part of the cost baseline, management reserves are also needed to account for risks that may happen and have not been identified. This amount becomes the total project budget when added to the cost baseline.

The project needs the money necessary to spend once a budget has been created and approved. Budgets are funded by organizations that specify how frequently increments of the budget need to be made available. For example, the frequency could be from "all at once" to "on-demand" to monthly, quarterly, or annually. The funding requirements may also specify the sources and other attributes of funds.

For example, a project manager we know used to manage projects to develop and install customized software packages for schools. Many school financial years run from July of one year to June of the following year. This timeline requires all projects to have estimates submitted by June. In June, the school sets aside or encumbers these funds. As projects progressed, the project manager would ensure monthly billing.

Running over budget was a huge problem – if this happens, the school administrators must meet to decide on the new amount. But these meetings are infrequent, and adding more money during the year might not be possible. So it was critical to have reasonable estimates and budgets upfront.

This book provides essential knowledge a project manager must have to avoid facing similar issues. Multiple chapters cover budgets and items that impact them:

- The Basics of Budgets covers terminology and fundamental concepts related to budgets
- Budget Presentation covers how to document and present a budget
- Project Financing and Project Payments explores financing terms and invoicing payments; they are planning considerations

Control Costs

Control Costs is how project managers monitor progress against the cost baseline and budget. The project manager needs to be sure to perform monitoring soundly. Simply subtracting dollars billed from the budget is not likely adequate for many projects. One notable San Diego project, the construction of Petco Park, found that by doing this, it was easy to be 100% spent when only half the work was done. Some sophistication and finesse are required to avoid issues.

The last section of this book is devoted to project cost management during execution, monitoring and control, and closure of projects.

Cost Management and Other Processes

Cost management processes touch every other project management process and knowledge area. Fundamentally, time is money, and these areas contribute to project costs. It is easiest to see this when looking at the project management knowledge areas.

Project Scope Management. Determining the proper scope guides team decision-making about the work to be performed. Knowing what work to complete guides the estimation process. The output estimates will form the basis for the budget.

Project changes will also add to costs. Therefore, change requests must include an investigation of the financial impact. Once changes are agreed upon, their costs must not be taken from contingency reserves but separately added to the budgetary requirements.

Project Schedule Management. The schedule is a roadmap for project completion, showing who does what and when. Information about resource costs includes the periods needed to factor into the budget.

Project changes will also change when resources are needed. So it is crucial to consider new costs and costs altered to meet a change request.

Project Quality Management. Just as time is money, quality comes with associated costs. As the demand for quality increases, costs increase as well.

It is not uncommon for project managers of knowledge-based projects (e.g., software development, technology) to neglect adding time and costs for testing resources. As a result, these projects often get stuck at 95% complete, consuming physical and financial resources. To avoid being stuck, exit criteria need to be clear, and compromises may be necessary to protect financial resources.

Project Resource Management. A thorough identification of project resources is necessary to get the best budget. In addition to acquiring resources, their operation may incur costs. For example, some operations may require sustenance over time (e.g., construction equipment paid for hourly and requires fuel). Therefore, another cost component is the period for which resources are needed.

Project changes also alter resource requirements, which add to the cost of change requests.

Project Communications Management. The generation and distribution of project communications add to project costs. Therefore, it is critical to add these to the project budget.

Project communications also need to satisfy stakeholder needs for information about project financial progress.

Contributions to Budget by Knowledge Area

Communi-cation	Integration	Procurement	Quality	Resources	Risk	Schedule	Scope	Stake-holders
•Cost of generation and distribution of communications •Documentation •Training	•Charter with budget goals and objectives	•Goods and services and their costs	•Increase or decrease in quality affecting costs	•Needed people, equipment, and materials	•Contingency reserve	•Timeline for resources	•Cost and quantity estimates •Change request costs	•Keep informed about budget •Approve budget

Table 1: Contributions to Budget by PMBOK Knowledge Area

Project Risk Management. Risks have positive and negative financial impacts on projects. These impacts play a critical role in determining project budget contingency reserves.

It's also crucial to consider that risk management activities will consume resources with associated costs. Therefore, include these activities and resources in project plans and budgets.

Project Procurement Management. Procurement encompasses all elements in a company's process of purchasing goods and services. Large projects often require separate procurement specialists to ensure required goods and services are in place during the progress of a project. Considering the procurement requirements and timelines early in a project helps plan and manage finances optimally.

One crucial planning aspect is when goods need to be shipped overseas. Depending on the country of origin and destination, import taxes and duties may add to costs.

Project Stakeholder Management. Stakeholders, including project team members, have valuable inputs to projects and, in return, expect to be kept in the loop on project progress. Likewise, stakeholders will have helpful information for budgets.

Project Integration Management. Project integration management spans all project process groups. Project initiation provides a project charter. The charter includes high-level information about the work and expected costs.

With the project charter as input, planning begins, and the Work Breakdown Structure may provide the initial cost estimates. As planning progresses, a budget is formed. During execution, monitor work progress and any changes, and it is critical to understand performance against scope, time, and costs.

Project closeout is a critical time and area where many project managers under-plan expenses. Development of training, documentation, acceptance test cases, health and safety requirements, and regulatory requirements all add to costs. Some of these costs may need to be carried over into operations budgets. And it is critical to provide excellent support as projects transition to operations.

Chapter Summary

- Four standard processes that are part of the PMBOK® Guide
  - Plan Cost Management – describes how to conduct cost management
  - Estimate Costs – use data to estimate costs
  - Determine Budget – assemble expenses into a budget
  - Control Costs – manage costs throughout the project
- Cost management integration – the connection of costs to other PMBOK Guide topics

Knowledge Nuggets

Chapter Pro Tip: The area of cost management requires more flexibility than other project management knowledge areas to conform to organizational norms.

In many organizations, cost management standards and practices are more influenced by existing norms, perhaps more than other project management knowledge areas. These circumstances, often created to support the Finance Department and their responsibilities to senior executives, lead to many variations in practice when it comes to:

- **Budget roles and responsibilities** – The exact role project managers play in creating budgets will vary.
- **What is included in budgets** – Some organizations include the reserves, others do not; some will require tracking of indirect expenses, and others will not.
- **How budgets are formatted** – Almost every organization has its unique budgeting format designed for senior management and the Finance Department.
- **Procurement practices vary greatly** –The variations often affect cost management practices.
- **Accuracy and precision of budgets** – Rules here vary considerably – one organization we know requires rounding to the nearest nickel, while most encourage whole numbers.
- **How to control costs and who controls them** – Control mechanisms and those with responsibility will vary.

It is incumbent on the project manager to consult with their management, Project Management Office (PMO), senior management, and finance professionals to learn all the rules and follow them. Citing standards and best practices will usually not help in creating change.

CHAPTER 2

PRINCIPLE: TIME VALUE OF MONEY

For projects, time is money. The money we have now is worth more than the same amount we may receive in the future. This principle is referred to as the *Time Value of Money*, which conceptualizes that today's money has earning potential to increase its value. This return plays a role in the selection and planning of projects.

Interest

Interest is paid to those who lend money and received by those who loan money or invest in other ways (e.g., purchase bonds). Simple interest is paid only on the principal (the amount that was originally loaned). In contrast, compound interest is paid on the accumulated amount of both principal and interest.

The amount of interest paid is based on many factors, including:

- Availability of funds

- Economic conditions (e.g., inflation, government intervention, current interest rates)
- Assessment of ability to repay a loan
- Time of the loan
- Liquidity of the loan

Interest received on investment is called "return," and interest paid constitutes the cost of borrowing money. It is essential for project cost management when deciding what projects to initiate and how to fund those moving ahead. Organizations may weigh whether to invest the funds or spend them on projects.

When the interest rates of fixed investments are relatively low, investments in projects are encouraged. Investment in projects is encouraged since a project may offer a better return than saving money. Lower interest rates also mean borrowing for projects is a relatively inexpensive source of funding.

Dividends

Stocks (and alternative investments such as mutual funds) are another form of investment that can earn a return or generate funds to invest in projects. A stock (also known as equity) is a form of security providing a fractional interest in the issuing company that is proportional to the amount invested. In addition, stocks pay dividends, typically quarterly, to investors. These returns are taken from corporate profits or reserves (i.e., money set aside to cover future obligations).

Unlike loans which are typically for fixed rates, dividends can vary. Not all stocks pay dividends; however, they all have an opportunity for growth in the stock markets. A good average return on stock investments (growth and dividends) is considered 10% or more for comparative purposes.

Future Value

The future value (FV) is what an investment will be worth after a certain number of years. Suppose we invest $1,000 today at 12% compound interest. At the end of one year, the investment will be worth $1,000 + .12*1,000 or $1,120. At the end of the second year, it increases to $1,120 + .12*1,120 or $1,254.

In other words, calculate the future value as

$$FV = (1 + r)^n * PV$$

Equation 1: Future Value

where **r** is the interest rate, **n** is the number of periods, and **PV** is the present or current value.

The formula can include multiple rates over an arbitrary number of periods, such as months and years. In this case, the power of various financial calculating software applications can assist in computation.

If all other factors are equal, favor projects with higher future values.

Present Value

Present value (PV) is the current value of funds expected in the future. A process known as discounting calculates the current worth. Assume, for example, that you will receive $1,254 in two years, including 12% interest compounded annually. Therefore, the present value must be less than $1,000 and can be calculated by removing the 12% interest received. Remove the interest by calculating the discount rate[2], which is

$$\frac{1}{(1+r)^n}$$

and multiplying the future value by it.

We can solve for the present value by

$$PV = \frac{1}{(1+r)^n} * FV$$

Equation 2: Present Value

where **FV** is the future value, **r** is the interest rate, and **n** is the number of periods.

Filling in the information, we find

$$PV = \frac{1}{(1+.12)^2} * 1,254$$

---

[2] For present value computations, the discount rate is the sacrificed interest if an investor chose to accept an amount in the future as opposed to receiving and then investing the same amount today.

Applying appropriate rounding[3], we find

$$PV = .80 * 1,254$$

Therefore, the present value is approximately $1,000.

Inflation

Inflation is a broad measure of purchasing power—rates of inflation rise as the prices of goods and services rise. Higher inflation rates reduce the ability to purchase goods and services and pay for projects.

Longer-term projects, those lasting 5-10 years or more, should consider the impact of inflation on the project. For example, one of the largest and most complex infrastructure projects undertaken in the US was Boston's Central Artery/Tunnel project, also known as the "Big Dig." The project lasted for more than 20 years, with some subprojects lasting more than ten years. Inflation accounted for a large portion of budget overruns throughout the project lifecycle.

The project's spending grew from US $2b to over $14b. The spending increase was primarily due to unanticipated increases in costs of labor and materials. "It is claimed that a major cost escalation factor on the Big Dig was inflation on all project elements lasting more than a decade, and the project management team reported that about half of the cost growth was caused by inflation (Greiman & Warburton 2009)."

---

[3] See Appendix B for Rules of Rounding. If this was an accounting or finance text, values would not be rounded. Project management is not as concerned with accuracy and rounding is usually appropriate.

There have been times when inflation has been historically low for many years, often less than 3%. However, project managers should not assume it will remain low throughout a project's life. Therefore, consider how salaries, fees, and costs will increase and accumulate over time when estimating and budgeting longer projects.

Chapter Summary

- Time is money for projects
- Money loaned as cash or bonds, is paid interest
- Stocks and equity are paid dividends
- Future and Present Value
    - Future value of an investment is what that investment will be worth in the future
    - Present value is the current value of funds expected in the future
- Inflation is a broad measure of purchasing power—rates of inflation rise as the prices of goods and services rise
- **Formulas**: FV and PV

Knowledge Nuggets

Chapter Pro Tip: Time is Money for Projects

Time is money for projects. The money we have now is worth more than the same amount we may receive in the future. It also means that money received sooner is more valuable than the same amount received later. The value is because we can either invest money in projects or financial accounts and expect a further return.

Rather than put all the eggs in one basket, so to speak, organizations will invest in a variety of projects or investment vehicles to protect the value of their cash. While bank accounts in our current economy are paying less than 1%, investments in stocks and bonds are still paying anywhere from 2-10% and higher. As a result, project returns from successful products may also be higher.

The time value of money creates a natural tension in the economy. Investments can increase in value. But on the other hand, long-term inflation can reduce buying power. Therefore, spending some cash now or more evenly over time may be beneficial. If possible, it also means that buyers and sellers will be motivated to hold some money.

Modern tools such as Google Sheets, MS Excel, and financial calculators will help ease the burden of computations formerly requiring interest tables. These tools and calculations are necessary as a point of comparison between potential projects.

Since time is money for projects, it is also essential for a project manager to reduce wasted time. The waste may range from padded estimates and schedules to "gold-plated" products (those which exceed scope and requirements) to ineffective communications. Learn more about the forms of project waste and do your best to reduce or eliminate waste in your projects.

CHAPTER 3

PRINCIPLES AND BEST PRACTICES FOR SUCCESS

Project managers need the most flexibility when dealing with project cost management. Some may never have budget responsibilities, while others may have partial or complete responsibility. Those with some duties will need to navigate many organizational practices dealing with issues such as:

- Financial policies
- Estimating practices
- Costs needed or excluded
- Budget formats
- Accuracy requirements

It is often incumbent on the project manager to determine these requirements and meet them. Therefore, it is essential to consult with your management, Project Management Office (PMO), if there is one, or finance professionals to learn more about requirements.

Here are six best practices that will help you achieve project success. They also apply to a wide range of cost management practices.

Cost Management is a Weakness

We know a project manager who recognized this weakness. He managed software projects with salaried human resources. For much of his early career, management did not require a budget. While without budget responsibilities, he studied accounting and finance and learned more about how his organization operated concerning budgets.

One day, management asked him to determine and manage the budget for a project undertaken to upgrade the networking infrastructure of all corporate facilities. Had he not been prepared, he might not have been given the assignment. To his surprise, this assignment became a gateway to managing a much more extensive program down the road.

Project cost management is an essential component of project management. However, many project managers possess no or limited exposure to budgets on early assignments. If you are one of these project managers, you need to acquire this essential skill. Although you won't need and are not expected to possess all this knowledge, map out a learning plan spanning over a year or more. In addition, it may be necessary to repeat some of this learning to absorb new practices when changing organizations.

Your Budget is Only an Estimate

Keep in mind that your budget is not absolute but rather only an estimate. It does not need to be precise (e.g., $1,100,456.35) and only within a specified accuracy (e.g., + or - 25%). You will probably revise your budget a few times before project execution. With each iteration, you will get closer to the final amount. A usual expectation is that the project's actual expense will be within 5-10% of that amount.

Where budget items are quantifiable, do the math and use the result. Also, include all the expenses, including fees, taxes (if applicable), and costs. Long-term projects may also need to consider the effect of inflation. After that, good estimating processes will guide you to an achievable budget.

A rate card specifies what an organization is willing to pay for specific resources. For example, Human Resources may publish salary or cost to company rate cards for particular titles and roles. Or a government agency may issue a rate card indicating the maximum amount they are willing to pay for specific materials. Determine if rate cards can either provide estimates or limit estimates for resources.

When we say, "the budget is only an estimate," it also means that you can drop the "cents" while discussing and presenting the budget to anyone. The knowledge and application of good rounding rules are also critical.

You Don't Always Get What You Want

Remember that the budget amount specified in the project charter can constrain some organizations. Therefore, you must reconcile the estimated budget to fit within that constraint.

Recall the story of the project manager we started talking about earlier in this chapter? When management considered the amount needed for the project, they called vendors and were provided quotes of a million dollars and up. However, they had not initially allocated anything for the project, so they decided to go in-house.

The first task for the newly assigned project manager was to develop a budget. Working with a consultant who helped with the project's designs, he managed to get it to $300k. Management was pleased but challenged him to reduce it to $250k.

So, the project manager returned to the team and asked them for alternative designs and ways to do the work. They found they could achieve $250k comfortably but could not go any lower without severe sacrifices. Management considered the rationale they presented and gave them the green light to continue, along with a promotion to program management.

Integrate with Other Project Management Processes

To develop a successful budget, at a minimum, work on scope management, schedule management, quality management, and risk management is required. These management areas will give time frames and costs to be factored into cost estimates and budgets. In addition, risk management will provide data needed to develop contingency reserves appropriately.

While these are the most common touchpoints, there may be more. For example, if project communications need a public relations campaign, the cost of communications management should be included. Similarly, if there is procurement, printing costs for a Request for Proposal may be needed. Therefore, as part of the budgeting process, go over each knowledge area carefully to see if there might not be additional costs.

Your New Best Friend

As a project manager, you manage by influence and not by authority. When it comes to working out some costs, this creates some challenges. For example, the Human Resources department will not provide you with specific people's salaries. Still, you may need to use some internal resources for your project. Some material costs may also be challenging to estimate.

Your organization's cost accountant can become your new best friend in these circumstances. Their job is to study costs, and they can often answer questions that others will not. For example, they may not tell you the exact salary of that programmer or electrician your project needs. Still, they can tell you their average cost. Then, when you complete your budget, they will also be one of the best experts to review it.

Check Variance Weekly

Some organizations may only require a status report fortnightly or monthly. Don't wait for the status report to review your budget variance (i.e., the amount you are over or under budget at any point in the project) - do it weekly. Checking at this frequency will reduce the time it takes to identify an issue and a solution and confirm the solution worked. The interval will often also help reduce the severity of the adjustments needed to get back in line with the budget.

In addition, you will need to monitor any variance trends. For example, has the cost-overrun been increasing week after week? Did you detect any big spike (outlier)? These conditions signal a need to analyze the situation carefully and determine if any corrective actions are required.

Chapter Summary

- Cost management is a weakness, so project managers need to plan to develop skills in this area
- Your budget is only an estimate, not absolute
- You don't always get what you want, so you may have to be prepared to modify the budget or scope or make other compromises to keep the project on target
- Integrate cost management with other project management processes
- Your new best friend, the organization's cost accountant, can assist with difficult budget and financial issues
- Check variance weekly for negative trends and outliers to determine if corrective actions are needed

Knowledge Nuggets

Chapter Pro Tip: Be sure that all agreed-upon changes include financial impacts, including those from new risks, then track these separately until there is an agreement to re-baseline.

Any changes to a project's scope may also impact time, resources, and costs, the traditional project constraints. So, before signing off on or declining a change request, be sure to analyze these impacts thoroughly. In addition to the possibility of new fixed costs, some resources, including their operational costs, may be needed for a more extended period.

It is also good to track and report these cost changes separate from your budget. First, it helps create a feedback loop for stakeholders to visualize the impact of requested changes. Then, fold these changes into the budget in the event of re-planning and re-baselining.

Finally, changes also need to be examined for risks. Any single change is usually not a good reason to change the contingency reserve amount. However, if there are many changes, a review may be necessary.

PART II: CREATING AND FUNDING THE BUDGET (INITIATION THROUGH PLANNING)

"It is easy to launch a project if you have no clue about the cost and schedule."

— **Gerry Geek**

CHAPTER 4

PROJECT SELECTION TECHNIQUES USING COST

Cost is a critical factor when considering which projects should be initiated and further planned. Therefore, getting the cost estimates as accurate as possible will ensure that the business can continue to start projects to meet strategy as soon as possible.

Note that cost should not be the only factor. For example, a new product may be necessary to maintain a competitive advantage. Organizations will need to develop the proper project selection criteria that function best for them.

A sound portfolio management system provides a single integrated solution to ensure the optimal mix of projects is always underway. The optimal blend should assure that the organization continuously improves, provides flexibility, and enables organizations to do more with fewer funds.

Once we have determined that a project will move forward, we should create a project charter. This project charter should state the high-level scope, budget, and resources and go into more detail if necessary. In addition, the project charter should name the project manager who will be responsible for project delivery. In many smaller projects, particularly in consulting or where time and materials contracts are used, we may use a more detailed contract in addition to the project charter.

The Project Business Case

A project business case is an essential document to aggregate and pass on the information and knowledge to develop a portfolio, program, or project charter. In addition, a business case should identify the value and benefits of the project for the project team and other stakeholders.

A business case should be considered a "living document," revisable as more information about the project becomes known. Depending on discoveries during detailed planning, some parts may need to be updated or refreshed. The business case should also be periodically reviewed and compared to project progress to ensure the promised benefits of the project can and will be delivered.

Often the organization undertaking the project will have its ideas of content and outline. The following paragraphs will outline some key content.

First, the business case should document the selected project or opportunity. Analysis of that problem or opportunity should include:

- How the solution contributes to and aligns with business goals
- The root causes of the pain or opportunity
- All the supporting analysis developed while examining the current and future state and identifying the gaps

- A highlight or summary of these gaps and the deliverables meant to satisfy them.

The business case also needs to contain information about the alternatives considered. The information developed may include assumptions and constraints, dependencies, valuations, and financial analysis to support decision-making and establish an initial budget and timeline.

Once the alternatives are laid out, there should be a clear recommendation. The proposal should include the analysis and rationale for the selected option(s), cost-benefit analysis, high-level milestones and product map, any dependencies between the work and existing work, and the roles and responsibilities needed to carry out the project's work.

Finally, the business case should provide evaluation information – how will we measure the project and know that:

- The resulting work conforms to all requirements,
- The resulting work is fit for use,
- The delivered product meets or exceeds expectations, and
- The promised benefits have been achieved.

Depending on your organization, other key content may be required, such as:

- Market and economic analysis
- Organizational needs and customer requests
- Strategic opportunities
- Technological advances expected
- Legal, environmental, regulatory, or other compliance required
- Social needs

Checklists and Scoring Models

Performing high-level or detailed screens requires a checklist or scoring model to ensure that all potential projects apply uniform criteria. However, checklists may be adequate for smaller, more straightforward projects. Checklists list the necessary, agreed-upon decision criteria and provide a qualitative scoring method (e.g., good, better, best).

Smaller organizations may use checklists to determine if the project cost management elements are appropriate for initiation. The list may include items such as:

- Initial cost estimated
- Budget and resources are available
- Project meets a strategic need
- Future profitability has been analyzed

Larger projects with more risk might add more details and assign weights to the criteria with a more detailed, quantitative scale to ensure a thorough analysis. Once the items are scored, potential projects are compared. Those that best meet the financial and non-financial criteria should move ahead.

Cost-Benefit Analysis

Cost-benefit analysis (CBA) or the Cost-Benefit Ratio (CBR) is excellent for comparing a project with alternative projects with similar goals. We may also contrast a new project against our current operation. Each alternative solution is evaluated based on what we must spend and our projected benefits.

Determining the costs and benefits will require detailed analysis to ensure we've included everything. Let's say, for example, we are evaluating imaging solutions to replace our paper documents. Examples of costs of our paper-based system might consist of items such as paper, file folders, cabinets, storage space, personnel time to manage paper and storage, and copy machines. The scanning solution would involve the costs of items such as scanners and computers, storage media, housing for computer equipment, and personnel to operate the equipment. We need to spend some time brainstorming all these potential costs.

Divide benefits into "hard" dollar benefits (measurable) and "soft" dollar benefits (non-financial or other benefits that are challenging to measure). For example, a hard dollar benefit of our scanning solution might be personnel costs saved in looking for lost documents. Compute the cost by determining the average time spent searching for lost documents and the personnel costs for the search. A soft benefit might be the more modern and up-to-date appearance we will give to potential customers who visit our facilities, generating more sales.

Once we've identified all the costs and hard dollar benefits, we can develop a ratio. Then, suppose two projects have similar proportions. In that case, we can look at the soft benefits and other factors to determine our selection. Finally, if conditions such as cost-benefit ratio and payback time are favorable, perhaps we should proceed with the project.

Looking at the ratio alone is usually not sufficient since two projects may have the same ratio but differ in costs by millions. We, therefore, need to make sure the selected projects will fit our budgets. We also need to be very careful to make sure we've included all the highest costs and benefits. It's often helpful to have a business analyst conduct the CBA and have a third party review the analysis to ensure an independent review.

Total Cost of Ownership

Cost-benefit analysis tends to focus attention on current project costs and future benefits. In contrast, Total Cost of Ownership (TCO) focuses on all costs associated with delivering the solution and the operating costs for the solution's lifetime. While some projects may be less expensive to produce, their future operational costs may be prohibitive.

The lifetime is typically three to five years for software and technology-related projects. If you are uncertain about the time, discussing the project with an accountant who handles depreciation would be beneficial since the useful life is closely related to depreciation.

For each period, deduct any hard dollar benefits or expected revenues from the accumulated costs to derive the ownership costs for each period. As with cost-benefit analysis, soft dollar benefits can support the analysis.

Cost Metrics

Cost metrics can play a role in project selection and planning for cost management. However, it is essential to note that cost should not be the only criterion. This section includes commonly used metrics to evaluate and compare projects. Is there one best? Unfortunately, not even experts agree.

Return on Investment (ROI). Return on Investment is used to estimate the probability of a gain or loss on an investment. It compares the investment gain to the actual investment.

$$ROI = \frac{Investment\ Gain}{Investment} \ x\ 100\%$$

Equation 3: Return on Investment

If we invest $1 and estimate we will earn $1, then the return on investment is 100%.

$$ROI = \frac{1}{1} \ x\ 100\% = 100\%$$

An investment with a higher ROI is preferred. However, one issue with the ROI metric is that it does not account for the time value of money. Therefore, it is more common for Net Present Value (NPV) to compare projects.

Net Present Value (NPV). The NPV is similar to the present value, but the calculation includes both costs and income. If t is the period and T is the total number of periods, then

$$NPV = \sum_{t=1}^{T} \frac{Cash\ in - Cash\ out\ during\ t}{(1+r)^t}$$

OR

$$NPV = \sum_{t=1}^{t} PV_t - Investment$$

Equation 4: Net Present Value

Therefore, projects with positive and higher NPV are more desirable and should influence their selection for a portfolio.

The PMP® exam typically focuses on the second form of the formula. An example problem might be:

> A small construction project with an expected $1m will generate $5m (in terms of present value) over ten years. What is the NPV?
>
> Solution: NPV – Investment = $5m - $1m = $4m

Internal Rate of Return (IRR). The internal rate of return measures the profitability of investments. IRR is the discount rate[4] (r) that would make the Net Present Value equal 0. Therefore, substitute 0 for the NPV and solve for r in the above equation. Due to the complex nature of the solution, it is best to calculate NPV and IRR using a tool such as MS Excel, which has built-in NPV and IRR functions.

Payback Period (PP). The payback period is the time it takes to earn back the project's cost (without considering the time value of money). Therefore,

---

[4] "The discount rate will be company-specific as it's related to how the company gets its funds. It's the rate of return that the investors expect or the cost of borrowing money. If shareholders expect a 12% return, that is the discount rate the company will use to calculate NPV (Gallo 2014). "

$$PP = \frac{Investment}{Annual\ Net\ Cash\ Flow}$$

Equation 5: Payback Period

Suppose $1,000 is invested in a project. If the product produced makes $500 per year for two years, the payback period for the project is two years.

$$PP = \frac{1,000}{500} = 2$$

Shorter payback times are preferred since that frees up funding to start additional projects more quickly.

Opportunity Cost (OC). Opportunity cost is about the "sacrifices made to gain some benefit (Pyle & Larson 1981)." While these costs are not a formal part of accounting, consider them when evaluating projects. For example, suppose we want to invest $1m in a project to improve plant and equipment. But, unfortunately, we need to reject that project to invest $2m in a new product to remain competitive. In this case, $1m is the opportunity cost of implementing the project to remain competitive.

Total Project vs. Portfolio Cost Risk

"When managing costs, we need to understand that underperforming projects may result in losses for the project and the portfolio. In the worst-case scenario, the company may fail if one or more projects fail. In the best case, the project adds value to the portfolio and another project. For example, a failing software project may provide code that another project can reuse. Or this may mean using an architectural drawing with some modifications for another project in construction.

Total portfolio risk is often referred to as beta or systemic risk. There is a systematic level of risk as the projects interact together. We need to understand that a high project risk does not necessarily mean a high portfolio risk. Let's look at a couple of examples.

Suppose an oil and gas exploration company has several projects to consider for drilling wells. The basics of each project include:

- The cost of drilling a well is $2m
- The probability of success is low – 10%
- Successful wells produce $24m revenue
- Unsuccessful wells are a 100% loss – ($2m)

Here we can see that if we drill a well, we could lose up to 100% of our investment if no oil or gas is found. We also see a low probability of success – only a 10% chance our well is successful.

But successful wells are enormous moneymakers. So, in this case, if we drill 100 wells, there is a high probability we will be profitable.

Expected Return = Expected Profit Per Well / Investment Required Per Well

=((Success Probability x Profit) + (Failure Probability x Loss)) /Investment Required Per Well

= ((.10 x 24m) + (.90 x -2m))/2m

=.30 or 30%

Doing the math, we see there is an expected 30% return. Therefore, high project risk is not equal to high portfolio risk. It is also true that as we diversify our portfolio, we can reduce risk, much as we do with financial investments. Further, risks that are not market-related typically do not affect the portfolio risk.

Now let's consider another, less calculated example. A grocery store typically has low beta risk (everyone needs to eat!) but wants to diversify by opening a computer store selling computers to small businesses. So, what are the project and beta risks in general terms?

Here we have a high project risk. A grocery store would have no expertise in the new business, and there are many competitors (e.g., Dell, Lenovo, HP).

There is a much higher market risk as well. The new business would be more susceptible to changes in the economy. And suppose the new company fails or suffers a significant loss. In that case, that could begin to erode the revenues from the core grocery business. So there is both high project risk and high beta risk in this case.

The Importance of a Basis for Initiation Estimates

Thriving and growing organizations have a continuous need for projects. Therefore, estimated needs for cash must be as accurate as possible. Also, there should be a basis for initiation estimates to achieve estimate accuracy.

Senior management must understand the need for accuracy. Any form of "padding" or addition of non-essential project elements should be discouraged at project initiation. Set aside project politics.

Consider if a manager at a prominent company made the following statement:

"I'm so excited! I needed $2 million for all my projects. I asked for $3.5 million and got $2.2 million. So I have $200,000 to play with this year (Morris 2010)!"

This attitude will lead to the delay of other critical projects within the organization. Having transparency in financial processes is vital to organizational success. Trust needs to be built between the board room and senior executives.

It is equally important to have a basis for projects completed for clients. One organization we're familiar with learned this the hard way. Both the organization and their client were large, multinational organizations.

A division of the client company called their local sales office for a quote. There was an interest in the entire company for the purchase. Upon learning this, headquarters called their local sales office to quote the same acquisition. The quote provided to the client headquarters was more than double the division's quote.

The salespeople making the quotes looked at their quotas and used them to derive each case's estimates. Now they were trapped – they could not explain in a rational way how the quotes were formed and lost a sale in the tens of millions of dollars. So an estimating tool was developed to help the salespeople explain why their quotes might differ within a year, preventing additional lost sales.

Chapter Summary

- A project business case is an essential document to aggregate and pass on the information and knowledge to develop a portfolio, program, or project charter
- Checklists and scoring models can provide high-level screens
- Total Cost of Ownership (TCO) focuses on all costs associated with delivering the solution and the operating costs for the solution's lifetime
- Cost metrics as a basis for project selection:
  - Return on Investment (ROI)
  - Net Present Value (NPV)
  - Internal Rate of Return (IRR)
  - Payback Period (PP)
  - Opportunity Cost (OC)
- Total portfolio risk is beta or systemic risk.
- A high project risk does not necessarily mean a high portfolio risk
- It is critical to have a basis for initiation estimates so you can explain them to others
- **Formulas**: ROI, NPV, PP

Knowledge Nuggets

Chapter Template: Project Business Case Template, Cost-Benefit Analysis Template

Chapter Pro Tip: When choosing projects to initiate and add to a portfolio, do not focus exclusively on costs.

Design and initiate projects to implement a strategy. As such, it is essential to understand non-financial reasons for projects. Focusing solely on costs may adversely affect strategy, such as creating poor quality products or failing to meet a crucial operational requirement.

Some non-financial reasons to initiate projects may include, but not be limited to, projects necessary to:

- Sustain or grow operations
- Remain competitive
- Increase efficiency and productivity
- Meet diverse stakeholder needs
- Refresh aging facilities or products

Costs are an excellent tool for choosing between similar alternatives. A lower-cost project may be the best alternative if all other factors are equal. Lower cost projects may also allow the initiation of more projects and help stay within the organizational budget.

CHAPTER 5

COST MANAGEMENT PLANNING

Complete detailed planning once a project is selected to move forward. Careful planning typically starts with a project plan which includes a section for each project management knowledge area, including cost management.

The cost management plan is not the estimates and not the budget (except for minor projects) but rather a description of how to formulate the estimates and budgets. When the document is complete, the team will know the essentials of how to be good financial stewards of their projects.

What is a Cost Management Plan?

The purpose of the project management plan, and hence the cost management plan, is to help the project manager guide the team to success. The plan establishes the procedures, methods, and measures for planning, managing, spending, and controlling project costs.

The best cost management plans are scaled to the size of the project and reusable. So rather than reiterate policy found elsewhere, either add value to it or refer to the policy. Generally, writing a good cost management plan for your first project will leave you with a reusable plan for future projects.

Critical Cost Management Plan Topics

For a complete cost management plan, consider the following sections (also in the cost management plan template) for a comprehensive plan that is appropriate for all but minor projects:

- **Title, Date, Author** – identifies the document and who is responsible for it
- **Document Control Information** – identifies updates to the document, when it was updated, by whom, and the updates made
- **Table of Contents** – where to find information in the document
- **Purpose of the Document** – brief statement of goals for the document
- **Roles and Responsibilities** – who will be involved in the cost management processes and areas of responsibility
- **Cost Management Approach** – a summary of the steps to be taken to create the cost management plan and how to establish and update the cost baseline
- **Cost Estimating** – information about how costs will be identified and documented, including
  - Techniques to be used
  - Work location(s)

- o   Units of measurement
- o   Accuracy and precision required
- **Budget** – how the budget will be created and reported, including
  - o   **Format** – how the budget will be formatted
  - o   **Currency** – the currency the budget will be in (best practice is the budget should be in a single currency)
  - o   **Costs** – how to determine them from the estimates and the categories that identify them
  - o   **Reserves** – which reserves are included or excluded (PMI suggests including only the contingency reserve in the budget, but not all project management methods agree)
- **Cost Control** – techniques for controlling project costs, including
  - o   How to track expenditures
  - o   How cost variance is measured, and at what frequency
  - o   How to treat unacceptable variance
  - o   Reporting formats and frequencies
  - o   Accuracy and precision of reports and other cost control measures
- **Cost Change Control** – how to make changes to the cost management plan and related documents (e.g., estimates, budgets)
- **Plan Approvals** – signatures of critical stakeholders to record buy-in
- **Glossary** – definition of terms and abbreviations
- **Appendices** – copies of any forms used and other supplemental information

Other Plan Topics

Almost no template is ready to use "off the shelf." While the critical topics include those necessary for virtually all projects, some areas may be specific to some projects and the industries in which they are performed. These projects may benefit from some of the following sections (and this is not an exhaustive list):

- **Prospectus** – a summary of project finances and financial benefits for senior executives and investors
- **Basis of Estimate (BoE)** – may supplement or replace some information in the cost management plan if a BoE was created (see chapter, Cost Estimation Techniques, for more details)
- **Tables of Rates and Costs** – if they exist, these could be inserted into appendices
- **Capital Budgeting** – how to handle capital budget items, including their acquisition and depreciation or amortization
- **Insurance or Bonding Requirements** – document any policies or bonds required
- **Resources to be Purchased or Procured** – any information needed for buyers or procurement specialists in your organization (detailed requirements may be in separate documents or appendices of the cost management plan)
- **Financing Requirements** – documentation of loans, including repayment terms and any bonds issued, including dividend schedules

Chapter Summary

- A cost management plan establishes the procedures, methods, and measures for planning, managing, spending, and controlling project costs
- Critical plan topics include:
  - Title, Date, Author
  - Document Control Information
  - Table of Contents
  - Purpose of the Document
  - Roles and Responsibilities
  - Cost Management Approach
  - Cost Estimating
  - Budget
  - Cost Control
  - Cost Change Control
  - Plan Approvals
  - Glossary
  - Appendices
- Other plan topics include:
  - Prospectus
  - Basis of Estimate (BoE)
  - Tables of Rates and Costs
  - Capital Budgeting
  - Insurance or Bonding Requirements
  - Resources to be Purchased or Procured
  - Financing Requirements

Knowledge Nuggets

Chapter Template: Project Cost Management Plan Template

Chapter Pro Tip: A good cost management plan can be helpful with edits for other projects.

Spending the time to write a good cost management plan can be valuable. A cost management plan includes many items which are not going to change over time or projects within an organization, such as:

- Estimation techniques to be used
- Budget policies, procedures, and formats
- Cost control methods
- Change control

Take the time on your first project to develop a plan, and then edit and re-use it for future projects. This strategy will save time while ensuring continued financial success for projects.

CHAPTER **6**

COST ESTIMATION TECHNIQUES

An estimate is an assessment of a quantitative result expressed in currency units. Estimates should indicate some detail about the precision or confidence in the estimate. But most importantly, estimates are best described as ranges. Therefore, an estimate for a project's overall costs might be $536m +/- $50m with 90% confidence.

It is better to count, measure, and compute – it gets the best possible result. However, there is always uncertainty when estimating, and there isn't always a single, correct answer. Therefore, we often derive estimates through rough and approximate calculations, explicit assumptions, or rules of thumb. For example, with assumptions and rules of thumb:

- Professional contractors hired for home improvements often provide quotes in dollars per square foot based on experience.
- Research has shown that computer programmers can produce ten debugged lines of code per day, regardless of the programming language used.

Reasonable estimates combine professional experience and judgment with independent reviews by experts. Use multiple approaches and estimators before merging the results into a final estimate. Estimation is a "team sport" – more heads in the game are better than one. Taking these steps will help to improve the accuracy of the estimate.

Estimates require validation. Use tools and techniques not used to create the estimate to validate it. These may include a rule of thumb, industry allocation methods, checking against historical data, or the collection of opinions of experts reviewing the estimate.

One easy way to validate an estimate is to determine the order of magnitude. An order of magnitude estimate will ensure the estimate is "in the right ballpark" by confirming that we are talking about 10s, 100s, 1000s, or more. Conversely, order of magnitude may make a good "first guess" at an estimate refined and validated by re-estimating with other methods. Collected estimation data may also be used to perform a Monte Carlo simulation of the project.

Every project should be estimated at least two to three times. Usually, an initial or sales estimate is created using top-down estimating at project initiation. Another good time to estimate is during project planning. Once detailed requirements are known, the high-level design is complete, or a detailed project schedule is available, perform another estimate. Additional estimates ensure that significant changes in scope, time, costs, or resources created during planning are included. The general expectations for estimating accuracy are as follows:

- Initiation estimate: -25% - +75% of actual
- Budget or plan estimate: -10% - +25% of actual

- Definitive estimate from requirements or high-level design: -5% - +10% of actual (PMI 2017)

Let's examine some standard estimation techniques.

Top-Down

Top-down cost estimates are estimates without details of categories or how the budget will be used. These will likely need to be broken down and detailed later. These estimates are typically created for project initiation by senior executives or others based on historical information, rules of thumb, or professional judgment.

A top-down estimate may also be a rough order of magnitude or ballpark estimate. These estimates are only expected to have the same accuracy as initiation estimates (i.e., -25% - +75% of actual). However, in addition to project initiation, such estimates may be helpful to validate that more detailed estimates are accurate (i.e., they are in the right ballpark).

Bottom-Up

Bottom-up estimates assess the lowest level of detail of the Work Breakdown Structure, usually the work packages. Then, aggregate the cost estimates of each work package to form an initial project cost estimate.

Bottom-up estimates are usually best determined by counting, measuring, and making reasonable assumptions. For example, if you are using a contractor paid $50 per hour to perform two work hours, the contractor is estimated to cost $100.

A critical risk of bottom-up estimation is missing work packages. Accurately determining all work packages at the beginning of a project is difficult, if not impossible. However, ignoring a costly work package will make the estimate inaccurate. Therefore, it is crucial to consider this risk when computing budget reserves (see the next chapter for Budget Reserve Planning).

There are times when other techniques are needed. Three standard estimation techniques to obtain a detailed estimate are:

Parametric estimates. Parametric estimates use historical data and statistics to determine costs. For example, suppose we are estimating a computer programming task. The developers estimate the job will take 100 lines of code based on a statistical analysis of past work. They are paid an aggregate of $1,000 per day. Combined with research showing that developers can produce ten lines of debugged code per day, the estimated cost is 100/10 x 1,000 = $10,000 (and developers finish in 10 days).

Analogous estimates. Analogous estimates use expert judgment to apply information from similar past projects to form an estimate. For example, a project manager is trying to estimate the cost for an architect to design a new building. The architect's rate is $100 per hour. Yet, last month the architect designed a similar structure in 48 hours for $4,800. The architect confirms that a similar design strategy and work are necessary for the new building. Therefore, the project manager estimates a cost of $4,800.

3-point estimates. Also known as a triangular distribution, 3-point estimates use three data points to determine an average. The three points are the optimistic (O), pessimistic (P), and most likely (M) estimates. The three points are added and divided by three.

$$Task\ cost\ estimate = \frac{O + P + M}{3}$$

Equation 6:Triangular Distribution or 3-Point Estimate

For example, if the time the $50 per hour contractor will work is uncertain, suppose in the

- Best case, the work is completed in an hour ($50),
- Likely case, the work will take two hours ($100), and
- Worst case, the contractor might complete it in four hours ($150)

In this case, our estimate is ($50+$100+$150)/3 = $100.

PERT

The US Navy, working with Booz Allen Hamilton, developed the Program Evaluation and Review Technique or PERT in the late 1950s. The goal was to improve the management of more than 10,000 contractors on the Polaris missile project (Wikipedia 2021). The emphasis of PERT is to control the schedule with flexible costs.

The basis of PERT estimation is the development of a weighted average using the most likely, an optimistic, and a pessimistic estimate. PERT estimates, also known as a Beta distribution, are superior to the triangular distribution that can overweight the pessimistic and optimistic estimates. PERT is ideal for innovative projects that manage risk by creating a more targeted estimate.

While PERT was designed for schedules, it can also estimate costs. Therefore, PERT is beneficial when evaluating projects where the costs are mostly related to human resources (e.g., hourly work) or are uncertain and difficult to estimate.

The fundamental PERT formula is the sum of the pessimistic (P), plus four times the most likely (M), plus the optimistic estimate (O) divided by six. Finally, perform the calculation for each task in the schedule and add the results.

To develop the range and confidence in the estimate, we need to look at the standard deviation. The standard deviation for each task results from subtracting the optimistic (O) from the pessimistic (P) and dividing by 6. While the reason is too complex for anything but an advanced statistics course, we cannot add the standard deviations. Instead, we look at the variance. Variance is simply equal to the standard deviation squared. When we add together the variances and take the square root, we get the number needed for the range.

The confidence level is one standard deviation or about a 68% confidence level. So if we double the square root of the variances, we have the confidence level at two standard deviations.

So to summarize, to complete the PERT estimate, we need to find the weighted average and variance for each task, then sum the weighted estimates. The range, positive or negative, will be the square root of the sum of the variances.

Suppose we double the square root of the sum of the variances. In that case, we now have the result for two standard deviations and are about 95% confident in the interval. In general, 95% confidence is sufficient for any project. When n is the number of tasks to estimate, the formula for PERT is

$$Cost\ estimate = \sum_{i=1}^{n} \frac{P + O + 4 * M}{6} \pm 2 \left(\sqrt{\sum_{i=1}^{n} \left(\frac{P - O}{6} \right)^2} \right)$$

Equation 7: PERT Estimation with 95% Confidence

Please see Appendix C: More About PERT for a complete example and a guide to using PERT to answer estimate "what if" questions.

Function Point Analysis

Function point analysis (FPA) is generally an excellent way to estimate when there is a body of experience with repetitive work. It divides the work into repeatable units that are approximately identical. Examples are easily found in software and construction:

- Framing and drywalling the rooms of a home
- Writing functions or subroutines
- Laying carpet or painting
- Installing network components
- Configuring software

Home improvement contractors will quote their work in terms of square feet of the improvement. Based on their experience with the average home, they know how many pieces of wood, carpet, and other materials go into a square foot of the average home improvement. Their knowledge will allow them to estimate time and cost based on the total number of estimated square feet.

Scanning the internet articles on Function Point Analysis, you will find a nearly exclusive focus on software. However, as can be seen, there are many applications.

Agile Estimates

The estimation of agile projects is very different from traditional estimating. Rather than determine specific times or costs, agile estimation looks at factors such as complexity, difficulty, and risk and compares each story relative to each other. As a result, projects requiring accurate cost estimates will likely not use agile estimating techniques.

The simplest form of agile estimation is t-shirt Sizing. Each story is rated as XS (extra-small), S (small), M (medium), L (large), or XL (extra-large). XS is generally for minimal tasks, like correcting a spelling mistake. XL means the story is an epic (a large story) that should break into stories that fit within one iteration. After discussing each story's relative complexity, difficulty, and risk, the team assigns the size.

A drawback for larger projects is that many stories fall into the same size category and are difficult to compare. Just as shirts made by different designers may have variations in size, ideas about the magnitudes of user stories will vary (Cohn 2013).

Another form of agile estimating that overcomes some of the shortcomings of t-shirt sizing is a game called Planning Poker. Poker Planning has more discussion and divides the stories up into more categories. These numeric categories are story points. Story points will help determine how the work progresses and how many stories will complete in an iteration.

With Planning Poker, each team member gets a deck of numbered cards. The numbers are usually Fibonacci numbers with some modification:

0, 1, 2, 3, 5, 8, 13, 20, 40, 100, and ? (unsure)

The larger the number, the more complexity, difficulty, and risk are associated with the story. Correcting a simple typing mistake in some text might be 0. Developing a simple logon screen might be 1. Securely storing a password with secure, unbreakable encryption might be 8. An epic, which would need a further breakdown, is typically assigned 100. More significant numbers, such as 20 and 40, might be used for more complex, challenging, and risky features.

During planning poker, the person responsible for the requirements reads and describes a story. Each team member then selects a card to represent their estimate before everyone reveals their selections together. Those with high or low ratings have an opportunity to explain their choice, after which the participants estimate again. Finally, the game continues until the team reaches a consensus for each story or epic (Mountain Goat Software 2020).

You can now see the cost estimation issues presented by agile projects. How, for example, is a large t-shirt size or story points of two translated to costs, and how is the budget known upfront? And if you are continuously welcoming new requirements, costs and budgets may continue to grow. An organization that needs to know costs upfront will not tolerate a budget formed by agile estimates.

Mitre (2022) suggests, "Estimating costs in an Agile environment requires a more iterative, integrated, and collaborative approach than in traditional acquisition programs. [...] Cost estimation on an Agile program is a team-based activity. [...] Ongoing collaboration among the users, development team, systems engineers, cost estimators, and other stakeholders is critical to ensure agreement on requirements prioritization in the product backlog and to gain a thorough understanding of the amount of effort required for each release. It also enables an integrated assessment of the operational and programmatic risks, technical performance, cost drivers, affordability, and schedules."

Basis of Estimate

A Basis of Estimate (BoE) is a document outlining how to create an estimate. The topics may include the logic and methodology used for the estimate. For example, if risks are factored in for cost estimates, this would be covered in the BoE.

There is no universal definition for a BoE document. The BoE most commonly contains the following:

- The work breakdown structure of the project
- Technical activities and their costs to meet the requirements of the project
- Any risks and extra activities that need to be done to mitigate risks
- Anything else that needs to be factored in (e.g., ramping up and rolling off staff as the intensity of the project changes, operational costs of resources)

The importance of BoE is that it does not merely take costs of elements into account but also factors in anything else that may impact the cost. As a result, this will be closer to the actual expenses than any planned costs that do not accommodate other factors.

A Cost Estimation Process

Estimating is not without its challenges. For example, it may be necessary for large projects with complex circumstances to have a team dedicated to the estimating process. Further, overall project plans need to include sufficient time to checkpoint the approach and project solution with the stakeholders before finalization.

There also needs to be adequate time for reviews with experts outside the project team but with solid subject matter expertise and a high level of project knowledge. Include time to develop a change of plans, if necessary, to re-plan part of the project. Perhaps the most difficult challenge is maintaining an environmental awareness of other project dependencies and managing multiple projects.

To be successful, develop an estimating process, follow it, and ensure it incorporates a review of an estimate. The following steps create a brief six-step framework for an estimation process:

Define. Start by defining the purpose and scope (what needs to be estimated) of the estimation required. The definition should include any ground rules, limitations, and assumptions. These should already be in the cost management plan for review.

Collect. Be sure to collect input from all relevant sources, including subject matter and industry experts with a high level of project knowledge. Other sources include the project plan, including the list of required resources. Where resource quantities are not yet known, be sure to understand the size and scope of the project overall. In addition, gather relevant information about costs, including rate cards or historical estimates from past projects.

Estimate. Prepare the baseline estimate. Consider all costs (e.g., taxes, fees, operational costs for resources) and economic factors (e.g., inflation, recession).

Analyze. Analyze risk information (e.g., the risks' Estimated Monetary Value or EMV) to determine appropriate contingency reserves. Consult management for management reserves.

Validate. Review and check estimates. For example, bottom-up estimates may be checked by rules of thumb, reviewed by experts, or re-estimated by another team. Estimates need buy-in from all stakeholders, from the executive sponsor to project team members, to succeed. Buy-in keeps everyone on the same page, working together for project success.

Post-Estimate. Once the estimates are complete, review and update the budget. Also, apply the right resources to the project with the proper skill levels and motivation to complete tasks within estimated limits. Suppose the estimate is not achieving project objectives. In that case, ensure that the level of effort isn't changed unilaterally. Project managers can bring in more resources and rearrange tasks first. Then, as a last resort, go back to the team to negotiate changes to effort and its impact on project success.

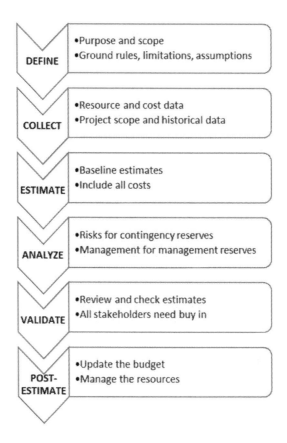

Figure 1:Estimation Framework

Repeat the process one or more times as more project details are known. Conduct lessons learned to improve future iterations.

Chapter Summary

- Top-down
  - Created by senior executives
  - Rules of thumb
  - Order of magnitude
  - Historical information
- Bottom-up
  - Parametric
  - Analogous
  - 3-Point
- PERT, a weighted 3-point average
- Function Point Analysis
- Agile estimates by t-shirt sizing and planning poker
- Basis of estimate (BoE)
- A cost estimation process
- **Formulas**: Triangular Distribution (3-point) estimate, PERT estimate

Knowledge Nuggets

Chapter Template: PERT Estimation Template

Chapter Pro Tip: Despite internet articles to the contrary, PERT and FPA can be valuable for many projects outside of software-related industries and not just for scheduling.

PERT estimation was a part of a more extensive system and was designed to focus on schedules. Its benefit is that it mathematically provides everything an estimate should have, including a range and a confidence level.

Often, schedules have uncertainty, so having three estimation points can address that. Costs have uncertainty as well and can be estimated by the same method.

Similarly, FPA was initially designed to measure the repeatable units of software projects (e.g., lines of code, functions and subroutines, and other code packages). However, many different types of projects in other industries have repeatable units. FPA can be applied to these projects as well.

Finally, don't fear mixing techniques. For example, US Patent number 7,801,834 B2 (Method and Apparatus for Estimating Tool) describes a system that includes an order of magnitude and function point analysis estimates with calculated ranges. It was designed to estimate software configuration projects with a limited number of potential configurations. Choose the estimating methods that best fit your project needs without concern for the industry or application they initially served.

CHAPTER **7**

THE BASICS OF BUDGETS

According to the sixth edition of the PMBOK® Guide, "a project budget includes all the funds authorized to execute the project. The cost baseline is the approved version of the time-phased project budget but excludes management reserves (PMI 2017)."

Unlike corporate balance sheets and income statements, project budgets usually are about expenses and not revenues. However, revenues are typically a part of the sales or product management process. Sales must meet revenue targets established by senior management.

Therefore, there are at least two cases where a project manager may need to estimate and monitor revenues (and other scenarios may be possible):

- Project managers in a dual project and product management role
- Project managers of self-funded projects (i.e., projects where the revenue of the first project phase fund subsequent phases).

What is a Budget?

Let's unpack the PMBOK Guide definition. The budget is all the funds that management authorizes for the project. At the end of planning, the cost baseline is the approved version of the budget. A large, complex project may be over multiple periods (e.g., quarters, months, or years). Still, more minor, more straightforward projects may have just a single period (e.g., five months) – whatever the length of the project will be.

Budget responsibility varies depending on organizational size and culture, project complexity, and assigned roles and responsibilities. Therefore, project managers need to be familiar with all aspects of budgets and treat cost management as one of the most flexible PMBOK Guide knowledge areas.

Managers of product development may be required to look at revenue. The revenue budgeting principles are very much the same as expenses. However, those managing products also need to trace money flow to defend their product.

For example, one project manager we know was denied funding to improve a product given to all users for free. Tracing how the money flowed, they found that half of the revenue of another high-profit margin product would be cut off if the "free" product didn't exist. They successfully secured the necessary funding to improve the product using that argument.

As this definition states, management reserves are excluded. What are they? Management reserves are funds set aside to cover the costs associated with issues created by unidentified risks of the project.

Include another type of reserve, contingency reserves, in the budget. Contingency reserves are funds set aside to cover the costs associated with issues created by the identified risks of the project.

Contingency reserves may be computed based on a rigorous risk management process. Alternatively, many organizations may set aside a percentage of the budget, usually under 25%, to cover the contingency reserve. We'll look at how to compute reserves and more aspects of implementing budgets in the remainder of this chapter.

Categorizing Costs

As you probably know from the book *Risk Assessment Framework: Successfully Navigating Uncertainty*, we firmly believe that having categories and prompt lists can help with brainstorming. While some budget estimates can be computed, a big part of the job is to ensure the inclusion of all costs. Therefore, it is critical to consider all the charges, including taxes, fees, and economic conditions. In addition, one or more of these categories may be required breakdowns of the budget.

Here are six different ways of looking at project costs to ensure they are all included and that your monitoring and controlling efforts are successful.

People, Equipment, and Material Costs. This first category is recognizable as the project management definition of resources. This categorization is excellent for identifying project resources and breaking them into three major categories. Be careful about accumulating all costs, including fees, operational costs, or taxes.

Direct vs. Indirect Costs. Direct costs are those directly attributable to the project. For example, they might include expenses such as salaries and training, special software or tools needed for the project, and materials such as lumber, nails, and chemical agents. Indirect costs are shared costs such as office leases for a headquarters building or shared copy machines.

Depending on your organization's financial and budget policies and practices, you may need to track some portion of indirect costs. Also, it is how the item purchased is applied and its relationship to the project that is important. For example, don't just assume leases are indirect costs. We've managed projects where particular work locations had to be leased just for the project - these were direct costs.

Fixed vs. Variable Costs. Fixed costs are those that remain more or less constant. For example, they might include the cost of a leased workplace or a fixed fee paid. Variable costs vary and may be more difficult to predict. In most cases, these costs are identifiable with language such as "per use" or "per hour." Therefore, it will be critical to have a solid schedule to estimate variable costs accurately.

Tangible vs. Intangible Costs. Tangible costs are costs of items that we can see, touch, or feel. Most project resources will fall into this category. Intangible costs are for costs of non-physical things, which are also more challenging to estimate. These costs might include project waste (e.g., wasted time, inefficient work).

Intangible costs, a subjective value placed on a circumstance or event, may also include items such as reputation or happiness. For example, unhappy project team members may not work efficiently, wasting more time. This wasted time may directly impact tangible costs, such as the time for which equipment is needed. Therefore, finding ways to keep team members happy will keep project costs down.

Deciding if an item is tangible or intangible will often require the assistance of a corporate accounting professional. For example, in both the US and the UK, there are circumstances where software (generally thought of as something intangible) may be considered tangible.

Operational Costs. Some equipment may cost money to operate. Costs could include fuel, electricity, maintenance, other sources of energy, and more. As you review your budget, include all operating costs for equipment and materials.

Sunk Costs. Sunk costs are those costs that have already been expended. These are also actual costs paid each period. While it can be emotionally tricky, do not consider sunk costs in making important project decisions. For example, suppose you spend $1m, only to find no way to complete the project successfully. In that case, the project should likely be canceled. Instead, find a way to make productive use of work already completed. Don't let that $1m already spent keep you from making the right decision.

Taxation

Taxes are compulsory financial charges imposed on individuals or businesses by governments. Taxes can affect both revenue and expenses.

Taxes on procurements are often overlooked when planning project budgets. Taxes may have various names, such as Value Added Tax (VAT), Goods and Services Tax (GST), or sales tax. They are often a percentage above the price of an item or a service procured. For example, if a machine costs $100,000, there may be an additional 7.5% VAT, making its total cost $107.500. Therefore, project managers need to capture appropriate taxes in their financial planning and management.

Certain taxes can be claimed back from the government, adding complexity. For example, if the 7.5% VAT paid for the machine is claimable, it should reflect on the project accounts. The company's accountant would be best poised to explain which procurements are taxable and which can be claimed back. Take care to identify them to manage project finances correctly.

Capital Budgeting, Depreciation, and Amortization

Capital budgeting evaluates investment returns in projects or other major purchases of plants and equipment, expensive licenses, or other significant purchases. These purchases are paid for immediately in cash or purchased with a loan. Still, the purchasing organization is permitted to recognize the expense of the asset over time.

By representing the expense over time, investment is encouraged. The encouragement happens through a compromise. First, the cost impact on the company balance sheet is lessened, enabling a more beneficial picture. Second, the period is determined by "useful life," an accounting concept.

Accountants determine the standards for useful life, and they are usually shorter than an asset's actual operating time. Computers, for example, are often written off over three to five years but can often be used in production for many years beyond their useful life. Once they are written off (i.e., all the expenses have been recognized), companies still have an operating asset. Therefore, they can invest in other needs, establishing a cycle of upgrades to plants and equipment that enable continuous improvement to the business's operations.

The expenses are usually recognized over time by a technique known as depreciation. Depreciation determines how much of the cost needs to be recognized every year. It is based on value loss from wear and tear or obsolescence. Project managers may need to track depreciation in project budgets or contribute to corporate financial statements (e.g., profit and loss (P&L), balance sheet).

Do not approach the complex capital budgeting and depreciation topics without discussing them with a finance or accounting department. In addition, accountants and various taxation agencies recognize more than two dozen different forms of depreciation. We will look at two, illustrated in the following table.

Assumptions: 4-year useful life, no salvage value	Year 0	Year 1	Year 2	Year 3	Year 4
Balance Sheet: crane	$500,000	$ 375,000	$250,000	$125,000	$0
P&L or Project Budget: straight line	$0	$ 125,000	$125,000	$125,000	$125,000
Balance Sheet: Software License	$500,000	$ 300,000	$150,000	$50,000	$0
P&L or Project Budget: sum of the years	$0	$ 200,000	$150,000	$100,000	$50,000

Table 2: Sample Depreciation[5]

---

[5] Year 0 represents a point in time when the asset is acquired.

In straight-line depreciation, subtract any salvage value[6] from the purchase price. Divide the remaining quantity by the years of useful life. Then, each year, equal amounts of the expense are represented on profit and loss statements (in the crane case, one-fourth of the $500,000 cost with no salvage value). We see the $500,000 asset on the balance sheet in the crane's year of purchase. In subsequent years, the asset's value is decreased by the $125,000 amount of the straight-line depreciation.

$$Annual\ salvage\ value = \frac{purchase\ price - salvage\ value}{years\ of\ useful\ life}$$

Equation 8: Straight-line Depreciation

The software license illustrates a "sum of the years" technique. In this case, a fraction of the expense less the salvage value is represented on the profit and loss statement each year. First, determine the fractions' denominator by the number of years added together (i.e., 4+3+2+1=10). The years in backward order become the numerators. So for the first year, 4/10 or 40% of the expense is represented on the P&L statement. After that, 30%, 20%, and 10% are applied for subsequent years until 100% of the asset is fully depreciated (Goodpasture 2004).

Amortization records the payoff of a loan for capital purchases or the lower value of an intangible asset (i.e., goodwill). When used for assets, amortization is approximately the same as depreciation. We will look at project loans further in the chapter, Project Finance.

---

[6] The salvage value is the value we can sell or trade an asset for when disposing of it, normally at the end of its useful life.

Currency Conversions

International business usually takes place in multiple currencies. If there are overseas suppliers, there is an option to make payments in their currency. However, avoid this unless there is an excellent reason. Overseas suppliers should be requested to send their bids and invoices in your currency and let the banks care about exchange rates.

In some cases, you may want to choose a globally-traded third country's currency to do your business. For example, suppose you are in Indonesia, and your supplier is in South Africa. In that case, you may choose the US dollar as the common currency for all your budgeting and invoicing.

In the rare event that you need to pay invoices in multiple currencies, you should request exchange rates from the finance department. However, your budget should be in one currency. Global companies opt to fix currency exchange rates internally for budgeting purposes (but not for actual payments, as this would be done according to the bank's exchange rates). However, if there is a significant fluctuation in currency exchange rates, the finance department may revise the internal exchange rates. If this happens, budgets need to be adjusted. The project manager should track these changes as part of managing costs.

Budget Reserve Planning

To start reserve planning requires a completed risk analysis[7]. First, estimate the financial impact for each risk, then compute the estimated monetary value (EMV). The EMV is the product of the likelihood and the impact in dollars or your local currency. Also, consider that risks can have both positive and negative consequences.

While it may have some shortcomings, one of the simplest ways to compute budget contingency reserves is:

$$CR = \sum_{1}^{n} EMV$$

where:

CR = Contingency Reserve
EMV = Estimated Monetary Value
n = Number of Risks

Equation 9: Contingency Reserve Calculation

Look at the hard dollar impact (actual costs) and any soft dollar impact (costs challenging to estimate, such as those generated by goodwill or change in reputation). Perhaps a large amount of money is not at stake. Still, the credibility as an organization is at risk, potentially reducing sales by a large but challenging amount to

---

[7] For details on how to complete a risk analysis, see our companion publication, *Risk Assessment Framework: Successfully Navigating Uncertainty.*

estimate. Therefore, do not add soft dollar impacts to the reserve but list them in support of the reserve.

It may not be unusual for some organizations to assign a fixed percentage (typically 5-15%) of the initiative budget for contingency reserves. However, good project managers will perform the actual computations and review them to avoid surprises later in the initiative.

Contingency reserve is different from the management reserve. Management reserve is not a part of the budget. Instead, it is the amount that management is willing to set aside for the unidentified risks. The estimate is usually determined by a top-down technique such as a rule of thumb or simply what the budget will allow. Management may elect not to share the management reserve and use it at their discretion.

Budgets and Rolling Wave Planning

Rolling wave planning is an incremental approach to project planning. With rolling wave planning, near-term work is planned in detail, while future work is only scheduled at a high level. As time passes, the plan continues to elaborate on near-term work further.

Rolling wave planning is ideal for long-term, complex projects, such as constructing an intranational, international, or transnational highway network. However, it can be used whenever uncertainty is in a project's key components, such as schedule and budget. It is also similar to how Scrum operates for Agile projects, where each iteration determines costs and schedules.

To be successful with budgeting requires several things. First, robust program management must be in place to ensure all the components and projects are operating and spending as effectively as possible. Second, this form of planning usually works best in environments where the budget is not a significant concern or regular funding intervals occur. Regular intervals enable funders and projects periods of reconciliation (Mill 2020).

Adaptive projects with many unknowns often necessitate rolling wave planning. On the other hand, rolling wave planning is usually unnecessary if a project is predictive. The important lesson is that if a project is short or budget accuracy is required, rolling wave planning is not a recommended approach. Furthermore, Agile is not recommended for these circumstances because of its similarity to rolling wave planning.

Chapter Summary

- Definition of budget
- Categories of costs
    - People, equipment, and material
    - Direct vs. indirect
    - Fixed vs. variable
    - Tangible vs. intangible
    - Operational costs
    - Sunk costs
- Taxation topics
- Capital budgeting, depreciation, and amortization
- Currency conversions
- Budget reserve planning
    - Contingency reserve
    - Management reserve
- Budgets and rolling wave planning
- **Formulas**: Contingency reserve calculation and depreciation

Knowledge Nuggets

Chapter Template: Depreciation Calculation Template

Chapter Pro Tip: Always seek management guidance and make friends with your cost accountant.

As we point out throughout this text, dealing with project cost management requires flexibility. Flexibility is needed because project finances need integration with the finances of the larger organization. Therefore, finance and accounting professionals in a finance department typically seek to have practices in harmony with theirs and meet their executive stakeholders' needs.

Some specific concerns to watch out for include, but are not limited to:

- Estimation requirements and techniques
- Budget requirements and formats
    - Mixed currencies and currency conversions
    - Reserves
    - Handling of indirect costs
    - Impacts of taxation and inflation
- Regulatory requirements
- Capital investment and expenditure requirements

To learn more about these practices, consult with your manager or Project Management Office. Consulting them will save time, and you will be able to develop your estimates and budgets the right way, meeting all needs the first time.

Cost accountants and other financial professionals can also be invaluable resources when learning about the organization, typical costs, and other financial data. Here are just three instances of how projects benefit from financial professionals:

- Salary estimates were needed to complete a budget, but the project manager did not have access to that data. Instead, a cost accountant supplied anonymous company data about the average salaries for various positions and skills that enabled the completion of the budget.
- A project was turned down because management did not want to invest in a free product. In addition, the project manager suspected that the free product was responsible for a large portion of revenue but had no idea exactly how much. Much to their surprise, a cost accountant informed them that the revenue generated was more than half of the company revenue. The project manager presented this information to management and the risk to revenue generated by not moving the project forward. The project received approval.
- A project manager with multiple projects for finance managers was asked to implement a simplified version of Earned Value Management (EVM) for status reports. The finance department told the project manager that bills that could provide actual costs were prepared for these finance managers on Friday mornings. The data could be made available to the project manager. This data enabled the project manager to implement a simplified EVM and meet a Friday status report requirement.

CHAPTER 8

BUDGET PRESENTATION

Having covered all the information necessary to identify and calculate all the possible elements of a budget, let's look at the different ways to present the information. But before we do that, just one more planning detail.

Suppose we are managing a waterfall or predictive project. A best practice is to associate the estimates with a Work Breakdown Structure; use a WBS Dictionary to record the cost estimates with their work package. If the project is agile, the closest analogy is the Product Backlog. At this point, assemble the estimates into the budget for presentation.

The Importance of Including All Costs

Assembling the estimates into a presentable format allows one to check for including all costs. However, a second look is critical since the expectation is that the final budget will be within 5-10% of the actual.

Some everyday costs to forget include sales taxes, fees, and operational costs for equipment. In some areas, sales taxes can be 8% or higher. Should taxable materials be a large portion of the overall budget, say 50%, you will have already used up your 5% cushion.

For longer-term human resource-intensive projects, economic conditions may also be significant. For example, if the workforce gets an 8% salary increase year-over-year, the cushion will be exceeded.

General Budget Best Practices

Perhaps an essential practice is always to follow organizational financial and project management policies and templates where available. Conforming will ensure your project is quickly reviewed and compared to other projects.

The basic rules for dealing with numbers in budgets are:

- Use a single, preferred currency,
- Use only whole numbers appropriately rounded,
- Enclose negative numbers in parenthesis and use a red font if available (as opposed to using the minus sign),
- Only use the currency symbol for the top and bottom items in a column or group of items in a column,
- Numbers greater than a thousand should include commas (or periods, depending on your locale) to separate thousands (the use of "accounting" format with no decimal places in spreadsheet software will address this requirement), and

- Writing (1m) or (1,000k) is far clearer than -1,000,022.53
- Single underline subtotals, double underline grand totals

Be sure to document all assumptions so it is easy for the reader to determine how various estimates were derived.

If you need to address revenues and not just costs, all the revenues should appear in a group first. Then, the costs will form a second group. Finally, each group should end with a total, and a net total, the expenses subtracted from the revenues, should be placed as a final item.

For a first draft, resist the urge to "tune" the numbers or solve problems by changing numbers, even with assumptions. Many decisions are best with team input – project managers should not make them unilaterally. Instead, let the first draft "speak for itself" as you present it to various stakeholders for review and have appropriate problem-solving and decision-making meetings.

WBS-Based Budgets

A budget is most easily formatted based on the Work Breakdown Structure (WBS). A simple two-column presentation is possible, with the WBS deliverables on the right and the budgeted costs on the left. In addition to getting the total cost, rolling up the levels in the WBS hierarchy provides additional subtotals. Be sure to add an item for contingency reserves near the bottom.

Once the budget is complete, some organizations may add accounts to the WBS work packages. These will aid in tracking the costs throughout the project while providing valuable financial information to management.

Budget for Project Team Breakfast				
WBS Level	WBS	Cost	Totals	Notes
Level 2	Bacon & Eggs	$ 60		8 dozen eggs, 4 1-lb packages bacon
Level 2	Drinks		$ 49	Drinks Total
Level 3	Orange Juice	28		4 gallons
Level 3	Tea	6		100 tea bags
Level 3	Coffee	15		30 oz medium roast coffee
Level 2	Toast	24		6 loaves
Contingency		$ 27		Assume 20% of budget
Level 2 Total			133	
Level 3 Total			49	
Project Total			$ 160	

Figure 2: Sample WBS-based Budget

Activity-Based Budgets

While a WBS-based budget is deliverable-based, an activity-based budget is based on project activities. Therefore, if a WBS with estimates exists, the first step is to develop a high-level schedule (if a schedule has not already been created) and allocate costs to activities. This strategy provides an additional opportunity to ensure consideration of all costs. The team can talk about work and costs, which may lead to discovering unnecessary work, previously hidden costs, work bottlenecks, and work efficiencies.

As with the WBS-based budget, a simple two-column presentation is possible, with the activities on the right, the budgeted costs on the left, and contingency reserves near the bottom. In addition to getting the total cost, rolling up the levels in the WBS hierarchy may provide additional activity subtotals.

Budget for Project Team Breakfast				
Activity		Cost	Totals	Notes
Cooking			$ 84	
	Bacon & Eggs	$ 60		8 dozen eggs, 4 1-lb packages bacon
	Toast	24		6 loaves
Serving			49	
	Orange Juice	28		4 gallons
	Tea	6		100 tea bags
	Coffee	15		30 oz medium roast coffee
Contingency			$ 27	Assume 20% of budget
Project Total			$ 160	

Figure 3: Sample Activity-based Budget

Other Presentations and Time-Phased Budgets

Many organizations have evolved budget requirements and templates to meet their own accounting needs. For example, they may be similar to WBS-based or activity-based or based on their categorization of resources. Rather than reinvent the wheel, it is best to check with your manager, finance department, or PMO before finalizing a template.

As the definition of budget stated, budgets are time-based. Simple, shorter projects may have a single period based on the project's duration. More complex, longer projects may need a budget breakdown by month, quarter, year, or business period. Time-based budgets may need the contingency reserves spread over the project's life or aligned with the last period.

Project Management Symposium Budget					
	Units	Cost per Unit	Amount	Year 2	Notes
Revenues					
Registrations	275	225	$61,875	$61,875	
Exhibition Hall Fees	35	50	1,750	1,750	35 vendors pay $50 per table
Platinum Sponsor	1	1,000	1,000	1,000	
Gold Sponsor	2	500	1,000	1,000	
Silver Sponsor	5	250	1,250	1,250	
Bronze Sponsor	8	50	400	400	
Pearl Sponsor	10	20	200	200	
Total Revenues			$67,475	$67,475	
Expenses					
Venue	1	1,000	$4,000	$4,120	
Hotel Rooms	10	199	7,960	8,199	4 nights for 10
Lighting Rental	1	450	1,800	1,854	for 4 days
Internet Access	1	200	800	824	for 4 days
Insurance	1	5,000	5,000	5,150	
Printing	400	25	9,800	10,094	
Printing Fee	1	75	75	77	
Reception	325	20	26,000	26,780	
Exhibition Hall	1	1,500	6,000	6,180	
Advertising	1	600	600	618	one time cost
Total Expenses			$62,035	$63,896	
Gross Profit			$5,440	$3,579	

Figure 4: Sample Time-Phased Budget with Alternative Format

Chapter Summary

- The importance of including all costs
- Budget best practices
  - Single, preferred currency,
  - Rounded whole numbers
  - Negative numbers in parenthesis
  - Currency symbol for the top and bottom items in a column or group of items in a column
  - Numbers greater than a thousand formatted by locale
  - Single and double underline
- Budget types
  - WBS-based
  - Activity-based
  - Other presentations
  - Time-phased

Knowledge Nuggets

Chapter Template: Budget Presentation Template

Chapter Pro Tip: Resist the temptation to fix budget issues by immediately raising prices or slashing costs.

When working on creating budgets, it is not unusual to discover issues. The issues may range from higher than expected costs or lower than expected revenues. However, project managers are problem solvers and need to approach budget problem-solving correctly.

I've seen many project managers that want to immediately raise prices to increase revenues or slash costs to meet cost targets. This approach is not going to get the best result. Increased prices may reduce sales, and slashed expenses may reduce quality or scope, creating unintended consequences. Instead, put together a first draft budget without changing the team's estimates. Then, take it back to the team and highlight the key issues that require a solution.

Facilitate the team in identifying multiple potential solutions for each issue. Aim for three to five and remember that postponing a decision or doing nothing are implicit choices. Then, list the pros and cons for each. Finally, reach a consensus as to the best solution. Now would be an excellent time to engage key stakeholders. Share the ideas with them and get their feedback. Then make a decision and create another draft budget.

A careful and thoughtful approach to all problem solving and decision making will lead to success. The success of the decision depends on:

- The diversity and quality of information and data available,

- The quality of the process followed, and
- The implementation of the decision.

CHAPTER 9

PROJECT FINANCING

Project financing is all about how project costs will be covered and paid. Depending on the industry you are working in, project manager involvement in financing projects may arrive sooner rather than later. As a project manager, you may also need to manage any costs associated with financing. This chapter aims not to provide challenging financial calculations or make you a project financing expert but to expose you to essential principles, concepts, and terms.

Consistent with one of the overarching themes of project cost management, project managers will need to rely on organizational financial experts from the finance department, the Project Management Office (PMO), or their manager for guidance on corporate policies, procedures, tools, and templates. Their advice is crucial for new project managers or those with first-time project financial responsibilities. In addition, as we have pointed out before, a cost accountant will help fill in any gaps in costs and local practices.

How are Projects Funded?

One way to finance projects is self-financing. There are three significant ways projects can be self-financed:

- Corporate income from operations is immediately spent on projects. This income often may be derived from agile projects that regularly deliver monetizable benefits.
- Projects may also be treated as capital expenses. Businesses retain earnings from prior years, and their treasury operations re-invest them in the business. Capital expenses may be allocated to acquire, upgrade, or maintain any owned property, buildings, or significant equipment.
- Projects may be cross-subsidized by other projects or programs in the portfolio. Cross-subsidies are common in the oil industry, where successful wells pay for unsuccessful wells and profit.

As an alternative, organizations may take out loans for project funding. However, projects financed by loans can be problematic if the project fails. Not only must the principal be repaid – interest will be due as well. In addition, some substantial projects are often based on unsecured loans or loans secured by future revenues. If these projects fail, the lender is also impacted and not repaid.

Project financing may add many pressures to the organization, project, and project manager. The funding must typically:

- Be in place, to start the project
- Consider that lenders are now stakeholders
- Not impact project benefits and value
- Consider cost control and cash flows

Interest payments from project financing may apply additional budget pressure, so explore financing considerations early. The time may be as soon as project feasibility is investigated or as initial concerns about adding the project to the portfolio occur. In general, projects may be financed by conventional or unconventional means, and we will examine these next.

Project Structures

Three unique structures for projects can affect financing and other aspects of cost management. While these are more common in the public sector, some non-public sector projects have adopted these models. The models are included here for completeness and must be a financing consideration.

Build, Operate, and Own (BOO). An interesting type of project is BOO, where an organization builds, owns, and operates an entity on behalf of someone else. Payments are received only based on the project's primary deliverable income.

These projects are common in the public sector — particularly with public-private-partnership (PPP) projects. Typically, a government would ask a private sector organization to build and operate a facility, such as an airport, and share the revenue from the airport. BOO projects are attractive for governments because public funds do not need to be invested. They are also appealing to the private organization that takes them up because it is usual to receive tax concessions.

Recently, BOO projects have become common in private organizations, especially in the telecom and hospitality sectors. In this case, one organization builds, owns, and operates a business under the brand name of another business.

Revenue from BOO projects starts generating once the project has moved to operation. As a result, there is always a sense of urgency to complete BOO projects quicker. Also, there is a tendency to be optimistic when planning. Project managers need to balance business needs (e.g., generating revenue as early as possible) and project needs (e.g., ensuring products meet safety requirements).

Build, Operate, and Transfer (BOT). BOT projects are very similar to BOO projects with one key difference. The organization that builds and operates the project's outcome must transfer it to the other entity within a specific period. For example, a government may ask a private organization to build an airport, operate it, receive revenue for ten years, and transfer it to government ownership.

This difference creates an even greater sense of urgency and more stringent revenue planning. Both BOO and BOT projects require very stringent revenue planning, determining whether expected project benefits are realized and the funding organization finds it profitable. These structures will have an indirect effect on the project manager. The project manager often finds there is a reactive tendency to cut funding if there are delays in the project. This reaction, unfortunately, leads to a spiraling impact.

Build, Lease, and Transfer (BLT). One way to mitigate the financial risk of BOO and BOT projects is the BLT approach. With this approach, the public sector partner (or the party which contracted out the project) provides a fixed amount of money to the party that built the project's outcome as a lease. The lease removes the private sector partner's risks. In addition, it reduces the pressure on the project manager, as the income would be predictable.

Conventional Financing

There are two primary types of conventional financing – equity and debt. Investors providing this type of financing include banks, investment firms, venture capitalists, shareholders, and suppliers.

Some projects may be financed by promises of equity or ownership in the project. Investors receive dividends or capital growth proportional to the percentage of their investment. Venture capital firms often fund technology projects and innovative products in return for part ownership in the company performing the project. TV shows such as Shark Tank and Dragon's Den have removed some of the mystery of how this type of financing works.

The contractors themselves may fund some of the projects in exchange for equity. For example, approximately 20% of the Eurotunnel or "Chunnel" financing was through equity granted to contractors and private investors.

Equity investments can be a higher risk for investors. First, their distributions can only happen after complete interest and loan repayments. For some projects, this can take many years. In addition, there are only returns if the project is successful. Should the project fail, the entire investment may be lost. As a result, investors providing cash in exchange for equity typically demand higher returns than others investing in projects.

Debt is a conventional form of project financing, usually in loans or bonds. Debt involves periodic repayment of the investment, with interest, based on agreed-upon schedules. Debt may be secured by cash or valuable assets, like how a home secures a mortgage. Debt may also be unsecured; however, there is a higher risk. For example, if the project fails, repayment of the lender or bondholder may not be possible.

Loans and bonds are senior debt. With senior debt, the borrower must pay off these types of debt ahead of others. Senior debt holders can also make the first claims on an organization's assets if a project fails. In addition, any debt secured must be repaid in any circumstances. If repayment is not possible, the lenders will take possession of the cash or assets offered as security. Since unsecured debt carries a higher risk, those providing unsecured debt financing often seek higher rates of return on their investment.

When a project fails or fails to deliver planned benefits, an organization may not pay its debts. The Eurotunnel, which was approximately 80% debt-financed, is one example – the early revenues were insufficient to pay off the debt. In this case, lenders may renegotiate to become equity holders. As a result, the Eurotunnel equity holders received a portion of future revenues, which helped offset some losses.

Another source of debt financing is loans from equity holders, which are also repayable according to predetermined rates. This type of debt is mezzanine debt. Mezzanine debt can only be repaid after all senior debt has been paid. Since mezzanine debt typically has more risk, it raises expectations for higher interest rates.

Unconventional Financing

Unlike conventional financing, there are many different means of unconventional financing. New ideas and new combinations of old ideas seem to spring up regularly. Let's look at some of the most common methods for unconventional funding:

Finance lease: Finance leases transfer the risks and rewards of ownership to the lessee. The lessor acquires the asset and provides it to the lessee for a fixed periodic payment. Project cash is freed by acquiring an asset for small, fixed payments. Given the temporary nature of projects, it often makes sense to lease any required working space for a project. The project may be long-term, or the facility may be used for operations later.

Finance leasing is also typically used when a project needs industrial vehicles or equipment. When the project completes, the asset may be put into operations with a new lease, or either party may sell it to pay off the remaining costs for the lessor.

Countertrade: A countertrade occurs when goods or services are accepted as payment. The recipient needs to sell the goods or use the services received to raise funds for the project. Countertrade is most common and popular for startups and international projects involving economically developing countries. The countertrade is beneficial when there isn't enough cash to finance the project and a commodity is available in excess.

When using forms of countertrade, it is essential to keep an eye on cash flow. However, cash is still necessary for operations, so too many countertrades can be harmful. There are six different types of countertrade transactions:

- **Barter**: Purchased goods are paid for by other goods. Barter is a less popular form of countertrade. It may not be simple to market and sell the goods received in place of payment or arrive at an agreeable exchange rate for the goods.

- **Compensation**: The goods offered in payment are transferred to a third party. The third party may either be a consumer or a seller of these goods. For example, this trade may be used in payment for another debt, used in operations, or the goods may be sold and the profits split.
- **Buyback**: This is the most popular form of countertrade. In exchange for providing an asset, say a factory, needed for an expansion project, the provider agrees to purchase or accept a certain amount of the factory's output as compensation for setting up the factory. Such agreements usually are for the long term and exceed the payment needed.
- **Counterpurchase**: This is a more complex but widespread form of countertrade. A counterpurchase is like a countertrade, except, in this case, the goods and services acquired are not directly used. Instead, they are sent to a third party for sale. In some cases, there may be an exchange that is like both a countertrade and counterpurchase. Again, some goods may be used, while others are sent to a third party.
- **Switch trading**: A company sells its obligation to another to purchase goods in a country.
- **Offset**: This is an agreement where one country purchases from another, subject to the project buyer purchasing raw materials and goods from the seller or agreeing to manufacture the product in the buyer's country (Wikipedia 2020).

International aid funding: The international transfer of cash, goods, or services, also known as foreign aid, can fund projects. While some transactions are driven through international banking organizations, such as the World Bank, some assistance may come directly from another country. For example, China's Belt and Road Initiative (BRI) invests in ports, buildings, airports, bridges, and other infrastructure projects in over 70 countries (CFR 2020).

Crowdfunding: This method allows many individuals to make small contributions to the overall funding, sometimes exchanging perks. Platforms such as Kickstarter take a portion of the funds as payment for brokering donations and projects.

Microfunding: Microfunding, also known as microlending, is where individuals loan smaller amounts of money to businesses without using a bank. Often services or mentoring are also provided, and the loans are provided with interest only, without fees.

The Cost of Financing

Debt and equity financing and many unconventional means of funding carry additional costs for consideration (e.g., interest payments). Consider these costs as they may significantly impact the financing decision. In addition, they may be beyond the project manager to compute, so be sure to consult finance professionals.

The cost of debt financing may consist of fees and interest rates. The availability of funds, security deposits, economic conditions, borrower credit rating, and repayment timing may affect these fees and rates. Credit card debt is typically the highest unless paid off within the allotted time. Note that the cost of debt financing is generally paid from taxed income.

On the other hand, equity financing is typically paid from untaxed income. The cost of equity is the dividends paid to the equity holders plus an estimate of the equity's growth. Equity may often involve giving up some control of the project or organization. Further, financing by equity and bonds may have other costs associated with them, such as payments to accountants, advisors, attorneys, and markets.

A combination of debt and equity may finance many large projects. In this case, the cost of capital is the ratio of equity times the cost of equity plus the ratio of debt times the cost of debt (Venkataraman & Pinto 2008).

$$\text{Cost of capital} = \text{Ratio of equity} * \text{Cost of equity}$$
$$+ \text{Ratio of debt} * \text{Cost of debt}$$

Equation 10: Calculating the Cost of Capital

Chapter Summary

- How projects are funded
- Project structures
  - Build-Operate-Own (BOO)
  - Build-Operate-Transfer (BOT)
  - Build-Lease-Transfer (BLT)
- Conventional financing
  - Debt
  - Equity
- Unconventional financing
  - Finance lease
  - Countertrade
    - Barter
    - Compensation
    - Buy-back
    - Counterpurchase
    - Switch trade
    - Offset
  - International aid
  - Crowdfunding
  - Microfunding
- Financing costs
- **Formula**: Cost of capital

Knowledge Nuggets

Chapter Pro Tip: Use these six tips to stay out of debt, whether business or personal, projects or organizations.

Review the budget. Carefully review the budget line-by-line. Understanding how you spend and earn is a critical first step in controlling debt. Be sure the budget is reasonably accurate, realistic, and up-to-date. The exercise will yield data to inform your next steps.

Increase revenues. More revenue provides more opportunities for paying off debt. One way to increase revenues is to increase sales. More cash will be available to pay off debt if you can drive more sales. In addition to increased sales effort, one way to consider driving more sales is lower prices. If you don't believe it will decrease sales, you can also raise prices.

Shorten payment terms. Time is money, so review the payment terms for your customer billing. Could the time to pay be reduced to raise cash more quickly? Now may also be an excellent time to check for any delinquent accounts.

Prioritize and consolidate debt. If there are many different debts, it will be vital to prioritize them. For example, it is common sense to pay back high-interest rate debt first. However, there may also be an opportunity to combine higher interest debts with lower interest rate loans.

Have a target debt. Goals and metrics provide a feedback loop that enables them to be met. By setting a target debt and measuring it monthly, you will be better prepared to manage debt.

Reduce expenses. Perform cost-cutting with care. Be sure that any reduced payment will not lead to negative consequences such as reductions in quality or loss of employee morale. It's usually best to look at the highest recurring costs first and minor one-time charges last.

CHAPTER 10

PROJECT PAYMENTS

There are many ways to structure payments, so our focus will be on those which can be identified upfront. Others may occur and need tracking as the project moves forward, but they will be challenging to identify upfront.

An example of this is construction claims. Claims are retrospective requests to cover costs incurred correctly but not covered in the original scope of work and similar issues, which may revolve around contract wording and understanding. For instance, in fixed-price or other contracts with cost ceilings, the buyer may demand changes, impacting the seller's ability to meet that price. These costs can be recovered through claims.

Common Project Payments

Cost reimbursement and reimbursable cost contracts are common forms of payments in projects. In their simplest form, cost reimbursable contracts are where contractors can bill for allowed costs plus an allowed profit. This billing is typically performed monthly, so contractors must know the allowable expenses and amounts expended each period. Likewise, the buyer will need to audit invoices more carefully to ensure that only allowable costs are included and the expected work and value are provided.

Incentive payments are often made to contractors for meeting specific targets, such as keeping within a specified timeline or budget amount. The budget may need to include an estimate of when incentives are paid or received.

Stage payments are payments due when certain stages or other defined work activities of the project are complete. They are often based on major WBS groupings. The project manager will need to consult the schedule for appropriate times to authorize these payments.

Many projects work on payment plans that include a down payment and additional progress or monthly payments until a certain percentage of the estimated project has been billed. Progress payments are typically based on milestones, so the project manager will need to consult the project schedule (and have a good one) for authorizing payments. Then, once the final project is delivered and accepted, any remaining payments are made and received.

While payment in advance is less common, some suppliers may require payment in advance at the start of the project (i.e., a down payment). Others may happen as needed (e.g., at purchase).

Invoice Payment Terms

Contractors and suppliers may include various invoice payment terms. The project manager must know what these are upfront.

With immediate payment required (also known as cash on delivery or due on receipt), the invoice should usually be paid within the month of billing.

Some invoices may include the language "Net x," where **x** usually is 7, 10, 30, or 60. The number specifies the number of days the invoice may be paid without penalty or interest due. The invoice or contract will determine what happens if that period passes and the bill is not paid. However, pay the invoice close to the due date without exceeding it from a time value of money perspective.

Modern payment systems and transactions often make it possible to schedule a payment within a specified time frame. For example, most bill-paying systems will withdraw the money and post the transaction overnight for participating parties. Payments are made within 5-7 business days to those not participating in the electronic exchange of payments.

Another payment form is x/y Net z, where **x** is a percentage discount if the invoice is paid within **y** days. Overall, the payment is due in **z** days. For example, a 2/10 Net 30 invoice means that I can take a 2% discount if I pay the invoice within ten days, and overall, the payment is due within 30 days. Here, some may be incentivized to reduce costs.

Finally, some invoices may be paid from a line of credit. In this case, payments may be automatic, usually within a month or quarter as specified by the line of credit.

Cryptocurrency Payments

Cryptocurrency is an alternative currency based on decentralized computer algorithms. The critical characteristic of cryptocurrency is that any single entity does not control these currencies. Unlike traditional currencies, governments do not currently regulate cryptocurrencies[8]. Initially, there was much skepticism around cryptocurrencies instead of conventional currencies (also known as "fiat currencies"). However, a few governments and organizations, including financial institutions, have started accepting cryptocurrencies as a form of money.

Market forces entirely drive the value of a cryptocurrency unit, and values can fluctuate drastically at times (unless they are currencies with exchange rates pegged to a fiat currency). Suppose any transaction needs to be done via cryptocurrencies. In that case, the risk of exchange rate fluctuation needs consideration during financial planning. In addition, many cryptocurrency transactions incur a separate transaction fee, which also needs to be included in estimates.

While this is an option for project payments, the best practice is to plan projects in one currency and require suppliers to provide their bids and invoices in the same currency.

---

[8] While not direct regulation, the US Internal Revenue Service currently taxes the sale or exchange of cryptocurrencies and the purchase or sale of goods with cryptocurrencies (IRS 2022).

Chapter Summary

- Common project payments
  - Cost reimbursement
  - Incentive payments
  - Stage payments
  - Down payments
  - Progress payments
  - Payment in advance
- Invoice payment terms
  - Due on receipt
  - Net x
  - X/y Net Z
  - Scheduled payments
  - Line of credit
- Cryptocurrency is an alternative currency based on decentralized computer algorithms

Knowledge Nuggets

Chapter Pro Tip: Due to the time value of money, pay invoices as late as possible without incurring finance charges, penalties, or other costs. And whenever possible, take an allowable discount.

Time is money, so there is an advantage to holding on to cash for as long as possible, especially during periods of high interest or dividends. Pay invoices as late as possible without incurring additional charges. Consider when to make the payment based on your payment method (e.g., online transactions are usually processed overnight, and checks are generally within five days). Leave a small cushion for unforeseen circumstances, such as mail delays or banking holidays.

It's also wise to take any available discounts – these are usually larger than interest rates. For example, if the terms are 2/10 net 30, take the 2% discount by ensuring the payment posts by the 10th day.

On the flip side, if you are billing someone, always send the bill as soon as possible. Prompt billing means sooner payment of the invoice.

While your finance department may dictate a change in mitigating circumstances, these are good rules of thumb to follow for professional and personal finance. Following this habit, you are always maximizing your investment and conserving cash.

PART III: MONITORING AND CONTROLLING COSTS (FROM EXECUTION THROUGH CLOSEOUT)

"Marketing and innovation make money. Everything else is a cost."

— Peter Drucker

CHAPTER **11**

TOOLS AND TECHNIQUES FOR COST CONTROL

As we start to look at how to control our projects out of cost allotments or face other issues, we need to understand there are only four basic actions. The project sponsor or client will play a critical role in determining which course we take. Outside of these four basic actions, there are other tools we can apply throughout the project life cycle to assist with cost control.

Depending on many factors, including project size and complexity, organizational policy, and project needs, you will have to choose one or more ways to track and analyze your budget. One method is to look at each line item and note the amounts that have been authorized, invoiced, and paid. This method is beneficial if you have a project with the procurement of goods and services. But most important, it makes sure there are no surprises. Other variance can come when estimates are higher or lower than the expenditure you authorize.

Longer-term, more complex projects also need to look at planned vs. actual expenditures weekly and periodic (e.g., monthly, quarterly). Any variance between these needs to be tracked. For example, a trend of over or under budget could be an issue that requires attention and possible corrective action.

Four Basic Execution Controls

When a project's budget is off track (overspent or underspent), there are only four essential actions to consider:

Ignore. If the problem is minor, ignoring it may be fine. A well-planned project has some tasks on, under, or at budget. In the end, these will likely even out and end with only a slight budget variance. It's more valuable to look at trends before taking action.

Correct: The two acceptable ways to steer an off-track project back to the original plan are through crashing (adding more resources) and fast-tracking (doing more work in parallel). Both courses of action introduce additional risk, and crashing adds extra cost, which isn't helpful for budgets. Fast-tracking is doing planned and budgeted work in parallel. From a budget perspective, it may be the best and only choice.

Re-plan: Here's where we may choose to change the project plan substantially. Actions may include everything from re-establishing the project baseline to de-scoping the project and agreeing to work not addressed now will be done in subsequent phases. Re-planning resets the baseline for all project parameters, including completion date, budget, and possibly scope.

Cancel: The project sponsor may just, at some point, admit to failure. Admission is often a difficult decision to reach. The sunk, already spent costs should not be a consideration. Instead, the project manager should consider using completed work to offset the loss.

Figure 5: Four Basic Corrective Actions

Feasibility Studies

Feasibility studies assess how practical it is to carry out a project. Feasibility studies can encompass technical, legal, operational, scheduling, and cost feasibility.

From a financial point of view, cost feasibility determines whether the project is financially viable. Determining feasibility is a proactive form of cost control, which takes the following into account:

- Total estimated cost of the project
- Estimated cash flow from the project's outputs
- Finance structure of the project
- Opportunity costs due to the project

127

The study should also include how the feasibility of a project would change under different scenarios, such as:

- Minor or significant increases in costs
- Minor or considerable reduction of a project's financial benefits
- External factors, such as changes in economic conditions

Feasibility studies provide the project sponsor clarity on whether a project should be undertaken. In addition, a feasibility study provides a tool for the project manager to approach cost control proactively under various scenarios.

Make vs. Buy Decisions

Make vs. buy decisions usually are made by management to either manufacture a product or project component in-house or outsource the work to a supplier. Project managers and project teams may influence or be asked to participate in decision-making. The process typically starts with a cost comparison of the in-house and outsourced goods.

As with feasibility studies, costs and cost-related objectives (e.g., to better manage cash flow or make an alternative investment) are just possible reasons to decide. Typically both quantitative and qualitative factors are considered.

Quantitative cost factors may include concrete goals such as achieving a specific unit cost. Qualitative cost factors may spread the investment over time or protect intellectual property. For example, over the last decade, Apple has increased its in-house chip-making capabilities to protect proprietary designs and have better control over costs and supplies (Gartenberg 2021). On the other hand, construction projects often outsource labor to keep overhead expenses lower and expand the labor pools.

Budget Control Charts

Control charts are tools used to detect and mitigate quality risks. Control charts may also manage budget variance to seek trends requiring corrective action.

Control charts show upper and lower control limits (the tolerance for variance) and how they are met over time. If a data point falls outside the upper and lower control limits, the budget is out of control or meets the Rule of Seven (and is also out of control).

The Rule of Seven states that if seven or more points are grouped consecutively together on one side of the mean, they are not random, and the process is out of control. Therefore, any data points from a Rule of Seven require an investigation to determine the cause of the variance. This investigation is a root cause analysis.

We can watch for other signals to make conclusions about the process. For example, we might see some unusual patterns in the data, such as ten days with hardly any variance and then a high variance for five days after that. It's possible that if we investigate, we will find some form of change on day 11 that led to this issue.

This example control chart measures weekly cost variance, measured in thousands of dollars. If the upper and lower control limit is set to +/- $10,000, this budget is still in control, and no corrective action is required. On the other hand, if the limits are +/-

$2,000, several weeks were out of compliance and should be investigated.

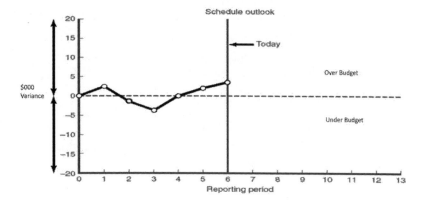

Figure 6: Budget Control Chart Example

Integrating Cost and Time

When making project budget decisions about resources, it's helpful to examine how the project's time and costs are progressing together. When plotting project time against cost, two shapes commonly emerge – an S-curve and a J-curve.

Many projects follow the S-curve. In this case, spending and the expenditure of resources start slow, accelerate mid-project, and then slow down again. Consider, for example, the construction of an apartment building. There is much architectural work, other designs, permitting work, and planning. However, not many resources are involved, and cash flows out more slowly.

After the slow period, work on construction finally begins. Multiple trades frame the building, provide wiring and plumbing, and close the walls. As a result, more resources and cash are consumed, making more visible progress.

As work nears completion, resource consumption and spending are slower. As a result, the finishing work, inspections, and finalizing plans to open the building for leasing take more time, and progress slows again.

In contrast, some projects follow a J-curve. These projects start slowly, build momentum, and finish rapidly. Example projects with J-curves are transformational and organizational change projects. As with S-curves, there is a slow start. Then, changes are implemented, and once things get moving, the project moves steadily to completion.

Figure 7:Project J-curve vs. S-curve

Decision-making does not require a detailed graph, just the general shape of the curve. For projects which exhibit S-curves, a top-down approach to budgeting is acceptable. Modest cost-cutting and a reduced level of resources will also be possible without significant impact.

On the other hand, J-curve projects will likely need bottom-up budgets. Any cost or resource cutting in the middle may seriously extend the project. Cost-cutting was the case with NASA's Space Shuttle Program, which fell three years behind, and then Congress cut the budget. The impact ended with the Challenger explosion in 1986 (Meredith 2017).

Project Financial Reviews

Conduct project reviews or audits to determine adherence to project management practices and the accuracy of various project claims about the project progress. Project financial reviews or financial audits may be a part of that process or completed independently. A project financial review or audit aims to determine adherence to the cost management plan and verify the accuracy of project financial information.

Status meetings and reports are frequently the norms for short-term reviews and reports. They are about the right information, at the right time, for the right people, in the right format. The project manager must work with stakeholders and develop a communication plan, including status reviewing and reporting.

Specifically for costs, the variance for the original (i.e., the baseline) plan should be determined. One minor glitch doesn't necessarily require action. Still, analyze a downward trend or a single large instance of variance to determine what steps need to be taken.

Conduct project or project financial reviews as small projects. They need to have explicit initiation, planning, execution, monitoring and control, and closing. Remember, the project team members may not see the "forest for the trees." An independent review team of design or processes experts might be required to examine everything entirely and objectively.

Project financial reviews may include mini-project audits. Those conducting the audit need to understand the cost management controls, examine project financial documents (e.g., budgets, budget reports, invoices, and payments), and assess control risks and accuracy of project financial documents.

The review needs to probe keenly and be "hands-on," meaning there should be site visits, questionnaires, interviews, and other facilitated meetings. Each review should end with lessons learned to ensure the review process is also improving over time.

Financial Regulatory Control

It would be impractical for us to cover all financial regulations; however, some facts are worth mentioning. First, the US and Europe lead the definition of financial regulations. Elements of their regulations may be found in many projects. Project managers should consult management and finance professionals to identify regulatory controls of concern.

Second, financial regulations impact projects in three distinct ways.

- The product or other result of the project may be subject to financial regulation, including economic sanctions.
- Financial regulations will indirectly impact how the budget and project financial reports need to be developed.
- Financial regulations will impact how the project may be financed, insurance requirements, and what occurs if the project fails.

Products in many industries in many countries are subject to pricing and other economic controls. Some notable examples include oil and gas, medical devices, and pharmaceuticals. As these projects are being initiated and planned, there needs to be a process to determine if the end product is feasible if subject to economic limitations. Pharmaceutical projects may also need to meet specific testing requirements, which add to costs.

The International Accounting Standards Board (IASB) developed financial reporting standards based in London. Their International Financial Reporting Standards (IFRS) are used in over 160 countries. These standards set rules for recording financial information, so it is of good quality and easily comparable from organization to organization (Investopedia 2021). The United States and China have similar regulations known as the Generally Accepted Accounting Principles (US GAAP) and Chinese Generally Accepted Accounting Principles (Chinese GAAP) (China 2017). These standards impact financial reporting, requiring support from budgets at the lowest levels.

Finally, local laws and regulations will dictate specific project financial parameters such as:

- Interest rates that can be charged or set,
- How money may be raised in particular markets,
- What happens if a project delivers but does not meet all contractual requirements, and
- What happens if a project fails or the organization enters bankruptcy.

While the previous forms of regulation mainly change infrequently, local laws and regulations may often change, including while a project is in progress. Therefore, project managers of long-term projects should check for regulatory changes at critical intervals, such as quarterly, annually, and when new project phases begin.

Chapter Summary

- Four basic controls
    - Ignore (and accept the consequences)
    - Correct
        - Crash
        - Fast track
    - Re-plan
    - Cancel
- Feasibility studies
- Make vs. buy decisions
- Budget control charts
- Integrating cost and time
    - S-curve
    - J-curve
- Project financial reviews
- Financial regulatory control
    - Generally Accepted Accounting Principles (US GAAP and Chinese GAAP)
    - International Financial Reporting Standards (IFRS)

Knowledge Nuggets

Chapter Template: Budget Control Chart Template

Chapter Pro Tip: Control waste. Educate yourself on the many forms of project waste that add to costs. Then, take steps to eliminate waste.

While often thought of as "lean," agile projects can be full of waste. This waste can lead to increased project time and cost, lower productivity, and a failure to deliver the value customers may be expecting. Much of the waste in agile projects comes from a desire for speed or time-saving. Still, often the time is only postponed rather than eliminated.

Waterfall or predictive projects may be subjected to similar forms of waste. These methodologies, however, often have built-in processes and procedures to address them. As a result, some waste may only occur if these processes and procedures are ignored.

A good project manager must learn to manage and control the following ten forms of waste (and solutions) often found in projects:

- Bureaucracy - red tape will delay the team; be sure to eliminate as much bureaucracy as possible without sacrificing necessary work.
- Churn - task-switching costs in overhead; reduce the need for multi-tasking to avoid excessive churn.
- Defects and rework - doing things right the first time is best.
- Delays - delays in obtaining resources and other delays add time to value production; identify and schedule all resources in advance.
- Gold-plated product - provide what the customer needs; resist the temptation to add "bells and whistles."

- Hand-offs - handoffs cause further delays and contribute to lost knowledge; organize work to minimize handoffs and closely monitor any critical path handoffs.
- Ineffective communications - as with all projects, communication is critical.
- Lost knowledge - with minimal documentation, necessary knowledge can get lost; be sure to capture all essential documentation.
- Partially completed product - incomplete sprints or scheduled work detract from delivering value; keep all work on track.
- Unplanned localization - not just for software projects, unplanned localization is time-consuming; consider localization needs during planning and not as an after-thought.

Take some time to review this list and consider how you will avoid these wastes for your next project.

CHAPTER 12

AN INTRODUCTION TO EARNED VALUE MANAGEMENT

Imagine you're the project manager for a project to lay four miles of highway in four weeks with a $1m per week budget. Now let's assume that only $2m was spent after three weeks. How is the project doing?

You might be suspicious because you have heard large projects always go over budget, but does this mean the project is doing poorly? The truth is YOU DON'T KNOW! Knowing how much money was spent is one piece of the puzzle, but how much work was done? Are there three miles of highway? Or perhaps only two?

If I don't tell you the cost but tell you three miles of highway are ready, you are no better off. Measuring project progress requires examining the triple constraint of cost, schedule, and scope.

To honestly know where a project stands (and apply proper project control), you need to look at the relationship between cost, schedule, and scope. These three are the standard, trackable project constraints (i.e., the triple constraints). Therefore, it would be best to convert each to standard units for an apples-to-apples comparison. Earned Value Management can help by converting all three to currency units.

Basic Concepts

In Earned Value Management, the schedule and scope are converted to dollars or other currency units to compare the plan to the budget. Once converted, it's possible to examine variance (i.e., the difference between the plan and the actual) and forecast project completion.

There are three basic terms to make this conversion, measure variance, and forecast costs and schedules. They are:

Term	Meaning
Planned Value (PV)	The value of work planned to complete in a period is measured by the budget for the work
Earned Value (EV)	The value earned is the budgeted cost of the completed work
Actual Cost (AC)	The amount spent to achieve the work that has already been done

Table 3: Essential Earned Value Management Terms[9,10]

Small, less complex projects can typically determine all the measurements accurately. However, larger, more complex projects

---

[9] PV was formerly known as Budgeted Cost of Work Scheduled (BCWS).
[10] EV was formerly known as Budgeted Cost of Work Performed (BCWP).

may elect to credit the value earned as a percentage based on the project completion percentage or other allocation methods.

Let's see how this works for our highway project. We will also assume the same level of effort has been applied weekly throughout the construction. At the end of the third week, the planned value (PV) will be $3m. So that's $1m for each week. The earned value will be the value of the work completed.

Suppose there were 2.5 miles of finished road. That would make the earned value (EV) $2.5m. The actual cost (AC), the money spent, was $2m.

Cost and Schedule Variance

To summarize, at the end of the third week, we have:

PV = $3m, the value of the work that should be done

EV = $2.5m, the value of the work done

AC = $2m, the money already spent

Now we can find our cost (CV) and schedule (SV) variance through two simple formulas:

CV = EV – AC, compares the value earned with the money spent, regardless of the schedule

SV = EV – PV, compares the value earned with the value planned to be achieved by now, regardless of the money spent

Equation 11: Cost and Schedule Variance

Suppose CV or SV is equal to 0. In that case, the project is right on target, and there is no variance, an improbable scenario. Any negative numbers are overruns (we're overspending on time and schedule), and positive numbers are underruns (we're underspending on time and schedule). For our sample project, the variances would be:

CV = $2.5m - $2m = $0.5m (ahead of budget)

SV = $2.5m - $3m = ($0.5m) (behind schedule)

Cost and Schedule Performance Index

While knowing the variance is helpful, we do not always need to act if it doesn't look favorable. Some project work will be early, and some will be late. Some work will cost more, and some will be less. We should be interested in large spikes or worsening trends.

Once we determine the schedule and cost variance, we can also compute the variance rate over time. The rate will help with understanding trends and making forecasts. We use the cost performance index (CPI) and the schedule performance index (SPI). Calculate them as:

CPI = EV ÷ AC, the ratio of earned value to costs

SPI = EV ÷ PV, the ratio of earned value to schedule

Equation 12: Cost and Schedule Performance Indices

In this case, a value of 1 means the project is right on target. Values greater than 1 are underruns, and values less than 1 are overruns.

Tip: It is easy to remember the variance and index formulas because they

- always start with earned value (EV)
- variance formulas use subtraction (i.e., -)
- index formulas change the minus sign of the variance formulas to a division sign (i.e., ÷).

Back to our example, we have:

CPI = $2.5m ÷ $2m = 1.25, an underrun

SPI = $2.5m ÷ $3m = 0.83, an overrun

These can be interpreted as:

We are getting $1.25 of value (125%) per dollar spent to be under budget.

We are getting 0.83 hours of completed (83%) per hour of effort spent to be over schedule.

Cost Forecasting

There are now a few more terms and formulas needed for forecasting costs. We will focus on costs to avoid complexity, and similar calculations are available for schedules. They are:

Term	Meaning
Budget at Completion (BAC)	The authorized project budget
Estimate at Completion (EAC)	What the total expenditure will be at the project's end
Estimate to Complete (ETC)	The amount of money needed to complete the project from the current situation
Variance at Completion (VAC)	The difference between the authorized budget (BAC) and what we forecast it will take (EAC)

Table 4: Additional Earned Value Management Terms for Forecasting

Suppose the CPI or SPI is the same over time. This lack of change is a warning that a past issue has not been corrected. So, in other words, we may be working at 125% of the budget, and we will remain at that rate.

In this case, compute the estimate at completion as:

EAC = BAC / CPI, the ratio of the authorized budget to the cost performance index

Equation 13: Estimate at Completion

The stated budget at completion for the project is $4m. Substituting the values:

$$EAC = \$4m / 1.25 = \$3.2m$$

The EAC means the expected total expenditure at the end of the project will be $3.2m, or $0.8m less than the authorized budget.

Also:

$$ETC = EAC - AC$$

$$VAC = BAC - EAC$$

Equation 14: Estimate to Complete and Variance at Completion

Again, substituting the values:

$$ETC = \$3.2m - \$2m = \$1.2m$$

This ETC means we need to spend an additional $1.2m to complete the project. And:

$$VAC = \$4m - \$3.2m = \$0.8m$$

The difference between the authorized budget and the forecasted end of the project is a savings of $0.8m.

Suppose the CPI or SPI grows over time or varies significantly. More severe issues may be involved, and there are better formulas to compute the EAC. In this case, other procedures can be used to calculate the EAC, but they are beyond the scope of this introduction.

These forecasts also allow the project manager to determine if catching up and meeting the original budget (or timeline) is feasible. The to-complete performance index (TCPI) compares the value of the remaining work to the remaining budget. TCPI allows us to determine if we can meet the estimate at completion (EAC) and the rate of change required to meet it:

$$TCPI = (BAC - EV) / (BAC - AC)$$

Equation 15: To Complete Performance Index

For the hypothetical project, this is:

$$TCPI = (\$4m - \$2.5m) / (\$4m - \$2m) = \$1.5m / \$2m = 0.75$$

To meet the EAC (which is lower than the BAC), we need to spend only 75% of the budget for the remaining time of the project.

Now, we need to compare the TCPI to the CPI. It should be easy to catch up if they are close in value. However, if the TCPI is greater than the CPI, the BAC may be understated. Similarly, if the TCPI is less than the CPI, the BAC may be overstated. However, unless there is an increase in the scope of work, the BAC must not change, so other variables must change to catch up.

Finally, the more significant the difference between the CPI and the TCPI, the less likely the project can catch up (PMI 2021). Furthermore, it may be impossible to catch up if this difference is not detected during the first 15% of the delivery schedule (Lewis 2011).

To conclude the hypothetical problem, since the TCPI and CPI differ by only .5 and there is a budget underrun, it should be easy to adjust spending to meet the authorized budget. But, of course, catching up would be less likely if the difference were more significant.

Chapter Summary

- Planned value, earned value, actual cost
- Cost and schedule variance
- Cost and schedule performance index
- Cost forecasting
  - Budget at completion
  - Estimate at completion
  - Estimate to complete
  - Variance at completion
  - To complete performance index
- **Formulas**: Cost variance (CV), schedule variance (SV), cost performance index (CPI), schedule performance index (SPI), estimate at completion (EAC), estimate to complete (ETC), variance at completion (VAC), and to complete performance index (TCPI)

Knowledge Nuggets

Chapter Pro Tip: If possible, use a simplified form of Earned Value Management for status updates. Stakeholders that appreciate detailed status will embrace these.

While the full practice of EVM may be very complex, it also provides a simple way to update clients on the status of smaller projects. But before we look at the "how," let's look at the "how often."

The frequency will depend on many things, but we recommend you start with once a week. If a month passes by and there's a problem, it's usually too late to do anything. Once a week allows you to keep closer track of expenditures and invoices. Once a week also lets the client see the progress. Of course, you can always skip reporting for a week if you didn't work on the project, but you still need to follow up on tracking expenditures and invoices. Log expenditures, invoices, and payments to see the complete project picture.

Your weekly client report needs to contain the basics of cost and schedule variance, plus an estimate of the remaining expenses. Knowing the cost and schedule indices isn't necessarily of interest to a client. Still, it's helpful information to determine project health. Rather than include it, you might use it in a formula to color code the data. A basic format to use for clients is:

	PV	EV	AC	SV	CV	ETC
Project 1	$0	$0	$0	$0	$0	$1.5M
Change Request 1	7,456	6,128	7,400	(1,328)	(1,272)	100K
Totals	$7,456	$6,128	$7,400	($1,328)	($1,272)	$1.6M

Figure 8: EVMS Status Reporting Format

Note that the projects and change requests are listed separately. In this case, a project hasn't started yet. However, a change request has. The condition might indicate that the client forgot something significant that the team had to complete before the project began.

The client sees the weekly progress of the planned vs. the actual expenditures. At the start of the status reporting, include a legend for the columns. A simple footnote under the table explains any significant deviations. Clients see what is happening from week to week -- there were no surprises.

You might improve upon this slightly by color coding based on the indices. Anything around 1.0 is good. Anything too large may be too good to be true, and anything less than .9 may indicate an issue requiring action. You can decide the actual performance specifications based on how tightly you need to control the project.

CHAPTER 13

CONTRACTS AND COST CONTROL

Our purpose here is not to provide legal advice or fully define contracts but examine them to the extent they contribute to cost control. While contract law differs from country to country, the basic principles of US contract law are generally more comprehensive. Moreover, they cover many regulations prevalent and applicable in other countries, though perhaps with some different shades of meaning.

Contract Basics

A US contract document must contain these elements to be considered legally binding, valid, and enforceable:

- **Offer** – There must be an offer made to provide goods or services
- **Acceptance** – The offer must be accepted

- **Consideration** – There must be an exchange of something tangible in return for the products or services. The deal could be money, property, or other services.
- **Capacity** – Those signing the document must be legally able to do so.
- **Intent** – There must be intent to enter a contract. The intent is usually evident when the agreement is written and the facts are correct as stated.
- **Object** – The object of the contract must be legal. A contract to purchase illegal drugs or provide services for illegal immigrants is not a binding contract.

While many legal systems permit verbal or implied contracts, this is not recommended in a project environment.

Other Contract Considerations

In general, all contracts should also include the following for clarity:

- The start date and length of the term for which the agreement will remain valid
- A detailed offer to provide goods or services and the details of pricing or consideration.
- Memorialize all promises in the contract – do not take things for granted.
- Any payment terms should be spelled out and include the mailing addresses for invoices and payments.
- Approved signatures of those able to bind the organization to a contract

- Agree on one set of rules if multiple jurisdictions with differing laws are involved

In addition, many contracts now include mediation or arbitration clauses to avoid the need for a lengthy court procedure.

Contracts may also contain some additional standard and special clauses to specify details of the agreement, known as terms and conditions. Terms and conditions can impact payments and costs, so project managers should know the ones in their contracts. Some standard terms and conditions include (but are not limited to):

- Acceptance: what constitutes acceptable work
- Bonds: purchased payment or performance guarantees
- Breach/Default: what occurs if obligations are not met
- Changes: how contractual changes may be made
- Confidentiality: what information can or cannot be shared
- Force Majeure: what happens in the event of an "act of God" (e.g., an earthquake)
- Incentives: additional payments for aligning with and meeting buyer objectives
- Intellectual Property: specifies who owns the work
- Notice: determines who receives contract communications
- Payments: detailed information on timing and amounts of payments
- Termination or Exit: establishes how a project can be canceled or abandoned before the contract is complete
- Warranties: promises of quality for goods and services, usually with limited periods

Regardless of your locale, contracts rely heavily on good faith, the good intentions of those entering the contract, and trust. When these are broken, following mediation or arbitration processes will help preserve the relationship between the parties.

Contract Types

There are four primary types of contracts, each with advantages and disadvantages. They are fixed price, time and materials, cost reimbursement, and incentive.

Fixed price contracts have their value agreed to and negotiated upfront. The buyer's advantage is that the project's budget is known upfront. On the other hand, sellers or contractors must carefully plan since they absorb the risk of delays and failure. As a result, the sellers will probably demand more project requirements and specifications before agreeing to a contract. The statement of work will need to have much more detail.

Failures of fixed-price contracts may mean complex negotiations. For example, a buyer could not comply with all the terms and supply everything they agreed to on time. On the other hand, the seller was hired for some specific expertise. They couldn't provide all the necessary resources at the specified times either. As a result, the six-month contract ran for more than a year, and then the seller returned to ask for more money. Finally, additional payment was negotiated, and the project was completed in 18 months; both parties were pleased with the results.

Time and materials contracts are generally best for short terms and are often used for staff augmentation purposes. Here the client or buyer absorbs the risk – they need to have the budget to cover the work and may have to negotiate larger budgets if the project work doesn't meet their needs. Many large enterprise software projects start as time and material contracts with a short-term expectation. Still, the implementations' lack of in-house experience and complexity usually makes for longer projects. The primary variant here is the labor hours, so the client needs to manage the work more closely to ensure all goals are met. These goals may include knowledge transfer to internal staff to reduce outside labor.

Cost-reimbursement contracts allow for payment of authorized and negotiated costs. These are often used by non-profits and facilities contracts such as building maintenance and service. They may also be used to specify research and development projects. The contractor or seller bears a lot of the risk and must have a sound cost accounting system to track the costs and make sure they are allowable. The client or buyer also needs to carefully monitor. There are several variants of this type of contract.

Note that a Cost Plus Percentage of Cost contract is not allowable for many government situations. When a vendor has their costs covered, plus an added profit for each expense, there is not sufficient incentive for the seller to reasonably control their costs. Adding an incentive, award (payment made on contract award), or additional fixed fee is more acceptable.

Incentives can come in many forms and should be designed to motivate the desired outcomes – they should reward positive and extraordinary efforts while discouraging waste. For example, a tight budget might incentivize meeting project financial goals. Those with shorter timelines may incentivize meeting specific goals or delivery targets.

Maintaining a specific date can also be important. For example, maintenance tasks may need to begin before the project ends (e.g., road repairs, repainting). They may require revenues to fund that work as soon as possible to minimize additional project costs.

There is no reason why there cannot be multiple incentives. Incentives may also be on a sliding scale. For example, the buyer may offer a 20% bonus to meet an exact delivery date or a 10% bonus for coming in a day or two earlier. For example, the Øresund Link built between Denmark and Sweden used multiple incentives and rewards to maintain a specific project end date over ten years. The project completion would coincide with an anniversary milestone.

Contract Selection for Cost Control

Familiarity with the basic contract types and their advantages and disadvantages are essential for cost control. Selection of the proper contract type can positively and significantly affect project outcomes. Procurement is much more complex and is a separate project management knowledge area. Still, correct contract choices will assist in meeting project cost goals.

You must work closely with your company's finance or procurement specialists to ensure projects are met—design successful contract negotiations to build relationships. Correct contract choices will help those in the relationship stay "on the same page" and achieve common goals.

Here is a table summarizing the advantages and disadvantages. Added incentives steer the outcomes further.

Contract Type	Advantages	Disadvantages
Fixed Price	• Less work for buyer to manage • Seller motivated to control costs • Total budget known up front	• Needs buyer to write detailed scope • Seller may not complete work if losing money • Seller may deliberately under price or under scope to profit from change orders
Cost Reimbursement	• Lower cost than fixed price since seller doesn't need to manage risk as closely	• Total price is unknown • Requires auditing of invoices creating more work to manage • Only moderate incentive to control time and costs
Time & Materials	• Quick to create • Usually short duration • Good choice for staff augmentation	• Seller profits from every hour, hence no cost or time control incentive • Requires most buyer oversight, but least buyer start up time • Total price may be unknown
Incentive (one of above with added incentive)	• Keeps everyone on the same page • Helps achieve goals and targets • The advantages of the chosen type	• The disadvantages of the chosen type • Additional cost to cover the incentive

Table 5: Contract Type Comparison

Chapter Summary

- Contract basics
  - Offer
  - Acceptance
  - Consideration
  - Capacity
  - Intent
  - Object
- Other contract considerations
  - Start date and length of term
  - A detailed offer and the details of pricing or consideration
  - All promises memorialized
  - Payment terms and addresses
  - Approved signatures
  - One set of governing rules
- Contract types
  - Fixed
  - Time and Materials
  - Cost reimbursable
  - Incentive
- Select contract type aligned with cost control goals

Knowledge Nuggets

Chapter Pro Tip: Contracts can reveal what aspects of the project are most important. Incentive clauses in contracts can keep everyone on the same page.

A well-written contract should reveal what aspects of a project are most important. The items of importance will usually revolve around one of the usual constraints of time, cost, quality, and scope. If you are writing a contract, consider adding an incentive clause or taking future actions to encourage meeting the most critical goals. If you are negotiating a contract, you may want to consider a request to add an incentive.

A perfect example comes from the construction of the Øresund Link, a bridge-tunnel connecting Sweden and Denmark. When the project began, the intent was to maintain an end-date ten years in the future to coincide with a celebratory day. However, through risk management practices, when the project was two to three years from completion, it was estimated that there was less than a 25% chance the end date would be met.

Normal schedule risk responses, such as searching for more work to be done in parallel, were implemented. In addition, the consortium managing the project offered a significant bonus that all contractors would share if the end date were met to incentivize completion. Finally, on 1 July 2000, the Link was officially opened, meeting the goal set ten years in the past.

CHAPTER 14

PROJECT CASH FLOW MANAGEMENT

The project budgets in an organization only tell a part of the story. Budgets are about when we will be making commitments of funds. But they don't tell us when actual cash is acquired or required for payments. Cash may need to be planned like resources for many large complex projects.

Cash Flow Concepts

For many projects, it is not just about costs and payments. For example, financing for large projects may mean that loan funds are distributed to the organization over time. Or suppose you are building a mixed-use tower. The customer may pay you, acting as the general contractor, a monthly amount in advance for some work. The idea is that these payments will help cover some of your expenses as you are running the project. Cash will both flow in and flow out.

Suppose you work for an organization that uses in-house human resources and has a central procurement department to obtain materials. In that case, this may not be a concern. But for large construction projects, for example, where most work is performed by contractors, not getting these plans and commitments for cash in place can mean the difference between success and failure. For example, if a contractor is expecting a payment and your Finance Department says, "sorry, we don't have the cash," the contractor may withhold some work or materials.

Cash Flow Forecasts

A cash flow forecast is time-phased, usually by month. It is an estimate of the actual cash required. Let's look at a simple example from your finances.

You plan to purchase a replacement air filter online for $20 in September and add it to your budget for September. You buy it on September 15 and decide to pay by credit card. You budgeted the purchase for September, but the bill is not immediately due.

Suppose you receive a credit card bill, based on your billing cycle, on October 10. It states that you have 25 days to pay without interest or penalty. Actual cash, therefore, is not required until November, when you pay the bill via your checking account.

Now let's look at a variation. You have the $20 for the air filter budgeted for September. A day before you purchase the filter, a friend gives you a $20 gift card for your birthday. So you have a cash inflow of $20. When you order the air filter, you enter the gift card number as payment, giving a cash outflow of $20. For the air filter, the net need for cash was $0.

By understanding money's payment terms and time value, you can think through every cost and determine the cash flow forecast. Having a good cash flow forecast will reduce business and financial risks. Companies need to look at cash flow carefully. Many have gone bankrupt, thinking only about the money coming in and not spending. At the same time, your organization will perform better financially, with each expenditure being more carefully planned and managed.

In the following figure, the net cash is negative, indicating that more cash is needed. A negative amount informs the need for a loan or to take funds from the organization's operations or treasury to cover the costs.

Cash Flow Forecast

Month	Cash In	Cash Out
September		
- contractor payments due		$50,000
- lumber purhase (down payment)		10,000
- August training courses		5,000
- progress payment received	20,000	
September Net Cash	($45,000)	

Figure 9: Sample Cash Flow

Chapter Summary

- Project payments affect the flow of cash
- Cash flow ensures cash availability
- A cash flow forecast is time-phased, usually by months
- It is an estimate of the actual cash required

Knowledge Nuggets

Chapter Template: Cash Flow Template

Chapter Pro Tip: Applying cash flow concepts to your personal and business finances will help you succeed.

Cash flow is a measure of the cash entering and leaving your accounts over time. Keeping an eye on cash flow will ensure that cash is always available to meet financial obligations such as debt repayment and operating expenses. Over time, strive to create excess cash. This extra cash can provide working capital for funding more projects.

Cash flow will also help you understand how funds are spent. The information will assist in creating better budgets and performing longer-term planning. Further, it will assist in putting money aside for future expenses or projects. Finally, watching cash flow will help determine the payment terms that should be given to buyers or clients to cover the expenses of providing them with goods and services.

So going forward, do not just think about revenue or profit. There have been profitable companies that have lost customers and suppliers and entered into bankruptcy because they were not properly managing cash flow.

CHAPTER 15

Cost Management and Project Closeout

Project managers are usually remembered by their project sponsors and clients for their project delivery and approach to closeout. Achieving a high level of satisfaction requires attention to many details, including:

- Ensuring that all requirements have been met and planning remedies if they are not
- Organizing acceptance test results and meetings to review them
- Documenting any known issues from testing
- Demonstrating the project and preparing for a turnover
- Seeing if the sponsor or client feels additional testing is necessary
- Preparing final copies of requirements, designs, training materials, user guides, operational information, and anything else promised
- Providing support during the transition period

Many project managers forget that each of these activities has an associated cost. If these activities are not planned and scheduled, it may be easy to exceed budgets during project closeout. In addition, project financial closure itself has associated costs for activities.

Project Termination or Suspension

Project managers also need to understand that a project may end in four different ways, and each may impact project costs. Therefore, consider the type of project termination when planning and executing project closure. These ways are:

Addition. Projects developed internally, yet independently, and successfully are made a formal part of the developing organization to play their role. For example, a university creates an extended studies division that operates independently yet is still a part of the university.

Extinction. A project succeeds or fails. A successful project achieves its goals and benefits and is turned over to the project sponsor or client for operations. Unsuccessful projects stop without meeting their goals. For example, a developed medical product does not meet regulatory requirements, cannot proceed, and the company decides it is infeasible to replan.

Integration. Successful projects are commonly embedded and integrated into the chartering organization.

Starvation. For various business or legal reasons, funds and resources may be withheld or withdrawn rather than end a project. After a period, the project may be terminated altogether. Termination by murder is a variation where the shutdown is quick and without warning.

Projects may also be suspended, a state which also implies costs. For example, if a construction project runs out of funding, the work may need to be halted temporarily. Work completed up to that point may need protection (e.g., a security guard, safe storage of unused resources) until additional funding is secured.

Project Financial Closure Planning

Financial closure consists of the steps necessary to ensure that all work has been appropriately completed and paid. Improperly performed, project financial closure can create legal issues involving contracts and payments. In some cases, a termination project manager is tasked explicitly with closing out the project. Therefore, the project manager should plan all financial closure activities during project planning. Omitting anything can cause a scramble during the last days of the project to close gaps.

Typical financial closure activities requiring cost and schedule planning include:

- Ensuring project sign-off
- Reviewing contracts for compliance and ensuring signed copies are retained
- Reviewing all invoices and payments
- Complying with any financing terms and transitioning from project financing to operational financing
- Identifying outstanding invoices or other required payments and arranging payment
- Receiving any final payments due
- Releasing resources at the earliest opportunities to avoid additional charges

- Selling unnecessary equipment and materials or returning them to an appropriate location or individual
- Ensuring any cost management issues are a part of lessons learned or post-mortems
- Conducting a final financial audit

Project Financial Closure

Financial closure offers immediate benefits. Legal issues are avoided, and the actual project cost can be calculated. However, all contractual and regulatory requirements must be met during the process. Therefore, now is the time to follow the closure plan carefully.

Project financial closure needs to be done entirely and promptly to avoid unnecessary expenditures. In addition, the project organization's finance department may be relying on the closure to make necessary reports, arrange additional financing for operations, and make adjustments to financial statements. So be sure to meet their requirements as well.

Once project closure is complete, it is best to have a final signoff. "This is rarely done in projects, but [we] strongly recommend having a specific close-out document, signed by both parties, that the contract [or project] has been formally ended and that all obligations have been met, except long-term obligations that are listed in the document, including post-project services and warranties (Lehmann 2019)."

It is important to note that the end of a project can be an emotional time for all concerned. Some people may be wondering about their next job. There may be a fear of ending friendships and other relationships, and the project may have become a way of life for many. While sensitivity is required, this does not hinder completing project financial closure.

Chapter Summary

- Project closeout activities
  - Ensure that all requirements have been met
  - Organize acceptance test results and meetings
  - Document any known issues from testing
  - Demonstrate the project
  - Prepare for a turnover
  - Check if additional testing is necessary
  - Prepare final copies of all documentation needed and promised
  - Provide support during the transition period
- Project termination or suspension
  - Addition
  - Extinction
  - Integration
  - Starvation
  - Suspension
- Financial closure planning
  - Ensure project sign-off
  - Review contracts for compliance
  - Review all invoices and payments
  - Comply with any financing terms
  - Transition from project to operational financing
  - Identify outstanding invoices and make final payments
  - Receive any final payments due
  - Release resources at the earliest opportunities
  - Sell or return equipment and materials
  - Ensure cost management issues are a part of lessons learned or post-mortems
  - Conduct a final financial audit

- Financial closure

Knowledge Nuggets

Chapter Pro Tip: Project managers are remembered for their delivery, so be sure to deliver financial success.

As stated at the start of this chapter, project managers are usually remembered by their project sponsors and clients for their project delivery and approach to closeout. Therefore, if financial success is critical to the client, be sure to deliver it.

Client needs and wants can take many forms. For example, we've worked on projects where financial considerations ranged from them being the most important to the least important aspects of the project. So at the start of each project, ask, "What does success look like to you?" to determine the client's specific goals and importance.

Some specific financial goals might include:

- Meeting the budget (within a reasonable percentage, usually 5-10%)
- Achieving specified savings through the use of the project result
- Earning a set amount of revenue with the project result

No matter the goals, be sure they are factored into planning, measured, and met when the project is turned over.

REFERENCES

China Briefing News. "China's Accounting Standards: Chinese GAAP vs. US GAAP and IFRS," May 31, 2017. https://www.china-briefing.com/news/china-gaap-vs-u-s-gaap-and-ifrs/.

Cohn, Michael. "Estimating with T-Shirt Sizes." Mike Cohn's Blog at Mountain Goat Software (blog). Mountain Goat Software, 2013. https://www.mountaingoatsoftware.com/blog/estimating-with-tee-shirt-sizes.

Council on Foreign Relations (CFR). "China's Massive Belt and Road Initiative," 2020. https://www.cfr.org/backgrounder/chinas-massive-belt-and-road-initiative.

Gartenberg, Chaim. "Apple Is Reportedly Going to Make More of Its Own Chips." The Verge, December 16, 2021. https://www.theverge.com/2021/12/16/22839850/apple-office-develop-chips-in-house-broadcom-skyworks.

Gallo, Amy. "A Refresher on Net Present Value." Harvard Business Review, November 19, 2014. https://hbr.org/2014/11/a-refresher-on-net-present-value.

Goodpasture, John C. *Quantitative Methods in Project Management*. Boca Raton FL: J. Ross Pub, 2004.

Greiman, V, and RDH Warburton. "Deconstructing the Big Dig: Best Practices for Mega-Project Cost Estimating." Orlando FL: PMI, 2009. https://www.pmi.org/learning/library/practices-mega-project-cost-estimating-6668.

Investopedia. "International Financial Reporting Standards (IFRS)." 2021. https://www.investopedia.com/terms/i/ifrs.asp.

IRS. "Virtual Currencies | Internal Revenue Service," March 11, 2022. https://www.irs.gov/businesses/small-businesses-self-employed/virtual-currencies.

Lehmann, Oliver F. *Project Business Management*. Best Practices and Advances in Program Management Series. Boca Raton FL: CRC Press, Taylor & Francis Group, 2019.

Lewis, James P. Project Planning, Scheduling & Control: The Ultimate Hands-on Guide to Bringing Projects in on Time and on Budget. 5th ed. New York NY: McGraw-Hill, 2011.

Meredith, Jack R., Scott M. Shafer, and Samuel J. Mantel. *Project Management in Practice*. Sixth edition. Hoboken NJ: Wiley, 2017.

Mill, Peter. "Utilising Rolling Wave Planning to Meet Funding Challenges." Association for Project Management, November 24, 2020. https://www.apm.org.uk/blog/utilising-rolling-wave-planning-to-meet-funding-challenges/.

Mitre. "Agile Cost Estimation." 2022. https://aida.mitre.org/agile/agile-cost-estimation/.

Morris, Rick A. *Stop Playing Games! A Project Manager's Guide to Successfully Navigating Organizational Politics*. Minnetonka MN: RMC Publications Inc, 2010.

Mountain Goat Software. "Planning Poker," 2020. https://www.mountaingoatsoftware.com/agile/planning-poker.

Project Management Institute, ed. *A Guide to the Project Management Body of Knowledge* (PMBOK Guide). Sixth edition. Newtown Square PA: Project Management Institute, Inc, 2017.
---. *Practice Standard for Earned Value Management*. Second edition. Newtown Square PA: Project Management Institute Inc. 2021.

---. *The PMI Project Management Fact Book.* 2nd ed. Newtown Square PA: Project Management Institute, 2001.

Pyle, William W., and Kermit D. Larson. *Fundamental Accounting Principles.* 9th ed. The Willard J. Graham Series in Accounting. Homewood, Ill. : Georgetown ONT: R.D. Irwin ; Irwin-Dorsey, 1981.

Venkataraman, Ray R., and Jeffrey K. Pinto. *Cost and Value Management in Projects.* Hoboken NJ: John Wiley & Sons, 2008.

Wikipedia. 2020. "Countertrade." Last modified May 24. https://en.wikipedia.org/wiki/Countertrade.

---. 2021. "Program Evaluation and Review Technique." Last modified November 5. https://en.wikipedia.org/w/index.php?title=Program_evaluation_and_review_technique&oldid=1053710479.

APPENDIX A

LICENSE TO USE AND MODIFY TEMPLATES AND INSTRUCTIONAL MATERIALS

Book buyers are granted access to tools and templates, provided "as is" and may be freely used and modified to meet their needs. But, of course, we always appreciate the recognition as the source of the templates. And for those who might need additional help, we offer training and consulting.

Please visit https://accidentalpm.online/downloads to access these materials. After registration, a process that takes thirty seconds or less, an account will be established, a link and password emailed to you, and the downloads will be accessible in your library. In addition, materials from our other publications (*Accidental Project Manager: Zero to Hero in 7 Days*, *Accidental Agile Project Manager: Zero to Hero in 7 Iterations*, and *Risk Assessment Framework: Successfully Navigating Uncertainty*) are accessible in the same online location.

Additional materials may be available for instructors who use this book for their classes. Materials include PowerPoint slide decks of lectures based on this book and experiential, project-based exercises for students. Once again, please feel free to modify them to suit initiatives. We appreciate at least a slide or a few sentences acknowledging the materials' source.

Please visit https://accidentalpm.online/instructor to access these materials. After registration, a process that takes thirty seconds or less, an account will be established, a link and password emailed to you, and the downloads will be accessible in your library. Please provide us with proof of the class and the text within 48 hours to maintain access. Provided proof could be through an online course or training catalog description, book order receipt, or other appropriate evidence.

If you do not receive an email with your account information, you can sign on at https://accidentalpm.online/login, use your email address, and click the "Forgot Password" link.

Need assistance with our site or meeting the specified conditions? Please contact us at support@ppcgroup.us or by using the contact page at https://accidentalpm.online/contact.

APPENDIX **B**

RULES OF ROUNDING

While estimates are supposed to include an estimate of accuracy (PMI 2001), scientifically doing this is difficult unless using multiple estimates, such as with PERT. On the other hand, estimates are already guesses – making an inaccurate guess on top of what may already be a guess would not provide the best estimates.

Generally, most project estimates, budgets, and other financial calculations can be done with whole numbers. Therefore, we only need to worry about the "cents" when paying bills and receiving payments.

Therefore, I recommend using appropriate mathematical rounding rules to reduce accuracy and give slightly more generous and understandable estimates. Senior management needs to know the project will be about $1m, not $999,999.98,

Four simple rules are:

1. One half or more rounds up, less than a half rounds down. Therefore, 4.499 rounds to 4 and 4.5 rounds to 5.
2. Do not use more precision than the least precise number. For example, when adding x.xx and y.y, the answer should be rounded to z.z.
3. Two decimal digits are appropriate when dealing with fractions representing percentages as they will be whole numbers as percentages. For example, 0.86 is 86%.
4. When dealing with a series of computations, round at every step.

When using Excel or similar tools for calculations, be careful. When using formatting to round, precision can be lost, especially if there are many varying length decimal numbers. Precision is lost because only the display is changed. Subsequent computations will use the unrounded value. Using the ROUND() function in Excel to round numbers properly is better. The function rounds the actual value, not just the displayed value.

Suppose, instead of Excel, a calculator is used. In that case, most calculators have a feature that allows all calculations to be performed with whole numbers or a fixed number of decimal points. You can use these settings for good rounding as well.

APPENDIX C

More About PERT

To start, let's look at a complete example. Let's suppose we have a project that has three tasks (A, B, and C). Further, the pessimistic (P), optimistic (O), and most likely (M) estimates for the task durations are known. Finally, only human resources work on these tasks, and their rates are known. Therefore, we can convert the schedule estimates to cost estimates.

The cost estimates have been provided (what the units are doesn't matter as long as they are consistent, but if it helps, let's consider these thousands of dollars). Our goal is to estimate the total dollars to complete the project with 2-sigma or approximately 95% confidence. The formulas are in the first row and last row.

TASK	P ($000)	M ($000)	O ($000)	PERT Estimate ($000)	VARIANCE
A	45	27	14	(P+O+4M)/6	$((P-O)/6)^2$
B	90	60	40		
C	45	44	39		
Total				$\sum(A+B+C)$	$\sqrt{\sum A+B+C}$

Figure 10: PERT Example

Now we can complete the chart using the standard mathematical rules for rounding (Appendix B).

TASK	P ($000)	M ($000)	O ($000)	PERT Estimate ($000)	VARIANCE
A	45	27	14	167/6=28	5^2=25
B	90	60	40	370/6=62	64
C	45	44	39	260/6=43	1.0
Total				A + B + C = 133	$\sqrt{25+64+1}$ =9

Figure 11: Completed PERT Example

The PERT estimate for the project is $133,000 +/- $18,000 with about 95% confidence. While it would be possible to continue doubling to increase the confidence in the estimate, going beyond 95% typically makes the range unrealistic. It will eventually encompass the entire budget (e.g., $133,000 +/- $133,000).

Now that the estimate is known, PERT has additional power. We can answer "what if" questions about the estimate using standard mathematics. These may be questions such as

- How confident are we if our budget was only $110,000?
- If we want to be 75% confident, what should our budget be?

We can answer these questions if

- the tasks are serial (one must be completed before the next begins)
- we assume each task is relatively independent.

If these conditions are accurate, we can assume that a normal curve distribution is possible.

Suppose we assume the odds are 50:50 that we can complete the project with the estimated $133,000. In that case, we can use a normal distribution curve to compute other possibilities. Fortunately, Excel has a function that can provide the computations for us.

If we want to find the confidence of a $110,000 budget, if D is the desired budget (110), M is our PERT computed budget (133), and SQRT(σ^2_μ) is the calculated range (18), then

$$NORMDIST(D, M, SQRT(\sigma^2_\mu), TRUE)$$

Equation 16: Excel Normal Distribution Function

Making the substitution and adding some other possibilities determines that if our budget is cut to $110,000, there is only 10% confidence in our ability to complete the budget with that amount.

Finish with budget?				Finish with budget?		
110	Normdist =	10%		180	Normdist =	100%
133	Normdist =	50%		190	Normdist =	100%
150	Normdist =	83%				

Figure 12: Applying the Normal Distribution Curve to Potential Budgets

Our example is a small project; however, the same principles apply to larger projects. For example, suppose we compute the probability for each task's cost estimate individually. In that case, we can multiply them together to determine the likelihood for the entire project.

Now let's look at the second question – if we know the confidence level we want to achieve, what should our budget be? Again, we can use the Excel NORMINV function to compute the funding required for any probability of success.

$$NORMINV (Probability, M, SQRT(\sigma^2_\mu))$$

Equation 17: Excel NORMINV Function

Substituting the values and again looking at other possibilities, if the client wants 95% confidence, we can complete the project with

$163,000. On the other hand, if 75% is "good enough," we could estimate the budget as $145,000.

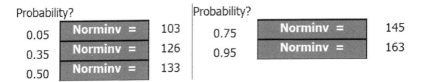

Probability?

0.05	Norminv =	103
0.35	Norminv =	126
0.50	Norminv =	133

Probability?

| 0.75 | Norminv = | 145 |
| 0.95 | Norminv = | 163 |

Figure 13: Applying the Normal Distribution Curve Inverse Function to Potential Probabilities

In conclusion, we have a mathematical means of improving the chances for success in virtually any situation involving the units of estimation (e.g., time, dollars) and the probabilities of reaching them. In recognition that we cannot demand projects to be risk-free, for our example, $150,000 with an 83% probability of success might be reasonable. On the other hand, if stakeholders had a strong desire to achieve the budget, $170,000 with a 98% probability might be appropriate. We know what we can negotiate for and have data to provide to stakeholders for decision-making using these techniques.

INDEX

present value 24, 25, 27, 47, 48, 53, 175

project charter 8, 15, 33, 41, 42, 53

public-private-partnership (PPP) 105

R

regulations 1, 16, 43, 90, 133, 134, 136, 151, 168, 170

reimbursement 117, 121, 154

return on investment 47, 53

S

S-curve 130, 131, 136

stakeholders 15, 38, 42, 57, 70–72, 90, 95, 100, 104, 132, 149, 187

straight-line depreciation 84

sunk costs 81, 89

T

tangible costs 80

time and materials 42, 154, 158

time is money 5, 11, 12, 21, 27, 28, 114, 122

to-complete performance index (TCPI) 146-148

total cost of ownership (TCO) 46, 53

transactions 109, 110, 119, 120, 122

triangular distribution 64, 65, 74

V

variable costs 80

variance 35–37, 57, 66, 125, 126, 129, 132, 140–143, 145, 148, 149

variance at completion (VAC) 145, 148

W

waterfall 2, 93, 137, 190

work breakdown structure (WBS) 8, 15, 63, 70, 93, 95, 96, 118

Accidental Project Manager
(Amazon Bestseller #1)

The perfect companion to the *Accidental Agile Project Manager*! Learn more about managing predictive or waterfall projects.

Each chapter includes a project management tip, reading selections from the PMBOK® Guide, and additional learning resources. In addition, a set of more than a dozen ready-to-use templates is available online.

Available in all Amazon marketplaces.
Paperback ASIN: 171879293X
Kindle ASIN: B07F714CMN
Audiobook ASIN: B093LKMTXR

Risk Assessment Framework
(Amazon Bestseller #2)

Ready for more project management knowledge? *Risk Assessment Framework* provides a complete framework and implementation recommendations to establish a comprehensive, reusable, and sustainable risk management methodology for any initiative. In addition, tools, templates, forms, and guidance support the framework's performance.

Whether you are an aspiring, new, accidental, or experienced manager, this book will help you successfully navigate uncertainty for any initiative.

Available in all Amazon marketplaces.
Paperback ASIN: 0989377075
Kindle ASIN: B07ZML9GW5

Accidental Agile Project Manager (Amazon Bestseller #3)

The perfect companion to the *Accidental Project Manager*! Learn more about managing agile projects.

Each chapter includes a project management tip, reading selections from the PMBOK® Guide, and additional learning resources. In addition, a set of more than a dozen ready-to-use templates is available online.

Available in all Amazon marketplaces.
Paperback ASIN: 0989377091
Kindle ASIN: B08L168NTJ
Audiobook ASIN: B09LYNV72D

BE A PROJECT HERO

Project Hero Academy

Your Roadmap to Project Management Success

- Qualified learners start free!
- Learn fundamental project management concepts & terms
- Take the training anywhere, anytime, on any device
- Earn your CAPM® Certificate in as few as two months
- Guaranteed to pass the exam

Upon completing Academy work, you meet your training requirement for the CAPM® certification and be prepared to take the exam.

Initial enrollment is free for qualified and motivated learners. We'll ask you to answer three questions to see if you are a good fit. So start your project management journey now!

Visit https://www.accidentalpm.online/project-hero-academy for details.

GET YOUR FREE TEMPLATES!

As a valued reader, you have access to all the templates referenced in this book and those accompanying our other books!

Sign up for access (you keep the downloads, plus they are in your online library) at:

accidentalpm.online/downloads

Bonus: Our PM Best Practices and Tips will be delivered once a month to your inbox.

Made in the USA
Columbia, SC
25 July 2023

20882780R00120